Hugh I. Strang

Exercises in False Syntax, and Other Forms of Bad English

For the use of teachers, and candidates preparing for departmental and

matriculation examinations

Hugh I. Strang

Exercises in False Syntax, and Other Forms of Bad English
*For the use of teachers, and candidates preparing for departmental and
matriculation examinations*

ISBN/EAN: 9783337409357

Printed in Europe, USA, Canada, Australia, Japan

Cover: Foto ©Paul-Georg Meister /pixelio.de

More available books at **www.hansebooks.com**

EXERCISES

IN

FALSE SYNTAX,

AND

OTHER FORMS OF BAD ENGLISH,

FOR THE USE OF

TEACHERS, AND CANDIDATES PREPARING FOR DEPARTMENTAL
AND MATRICULATION EXAMINATIONS.

BY

H. I. STRANG, B.A.

HEAD MASTER, GODERICH HIGH SCHOOL.

———

PREFACE.

In laying before my fellow-teachers this collection of Exercises in False Syntax, and other forms of bad English, it may not be amiss for me to say a few words in regard to its origin and its object.

I had not been long engaged in High School work before I discovered that in very many cases pupils who had a ready command of grammatical rules and definitions, and who were fairly proficient in analysis and parsing, were, yet, seemingly unable to detect common and undoubted errors in sentences in every-day use. Further experience showed me that even after they had learned to notice and correct mistakes in sentences given them for that purpose, many of them would continue to make the same or similar mistakes in their ordinary speaking and writing. I was led to conclude, therefore, that, accustomed as the majority of our pupils are, from childhood, to hearing incorrect forms of speech used by those around them, special and systematic drill is necessary to teach them to notice and guard against these wrong forms ; and that this drill should be oral as well as written, in order that both the ear and the eye may be enlisted in the cause of good English, and trained to assist the student.

Holding this opinion, and not finding in any of our text-books a suitable collection of exercises for such drill, I began to compile one, and this book is the result of my labors. Whether other teachers have felt the same want, and whether, if so, this collection will meet it, is for them to say. I hardly expect that it will prove wholly satisfactory to any one, but, nevertheless, I have been encouraged to believe that it will be found sufficiently comprehensive and practical to be of some service. It is not intended to take the place of any other book, nor has it been prepared to suit any particular work on Grammar or Composition. My plan has been to give under each heading examples of all the common, typical errors of that class, and then by frequent review exercises to accustom the student to be on his guard at all points. I have inserted, also, a a few sets of questions bearing directly on the correct use of different forms of expression. While. however. I have endeavored to include examples of all common errors, I need scarcely say that teachers may find it necessary to drill particularly and repeatedly on certain points, and for that purpose may have to supplement the exercises I have given ; and that in some localities it may also be necessary to add a few dialectic or provincial forms of expression. In fact, any teacher who will take the trouble to note down from day to day words and sentences which he hears or sees in his school work, can make for himself a better collection of examples for oral drill than any book can furnish him.

A few of the examples have been selected from text-books and examination papers ; a few more have been kindly contributed by friends or pupils ; the rest have been gathered at intervals from a great variety of sources. As my object is to call attention to the mistakes, and not to the persons who have made them, I have not thought it either necessary or wise to give any references ; and should any one on looking through the book find that he has been an unintentional contributor to its pages, I trust he will not take offence, but rather be glad that his mistakes are being put to so good a use. I have not spared my own blunders, and have, therefore, felt less hesitation in availing myself of those of others.

In conclusion I wish to say that I shall be glad to receive any criticisms or suggestions, in order that if a second edition should ever be called for, I may be able to make the book more useful.

GODERICH, August, 1883.

PREFACE TO THE SECOND EDITION.

A second Edition having been called for much sooner than I expected, I find myself unable, without unduly delaying the publishers, to do more in the way of adding to the usefulness of the book than to correct such errors as I noticed in the first edition, and to add a few examples to some of the exercises in Part III.

January, 1884.

TABLE OF CONTENTS.

PART I.
ACCIDENCE.

PART II.
SYNTAX.

PART III.

STYLE.

PART I.

ACCIDENCE.

NOUNS.

I.—WRONG PLURAL FORMS.
II.—WRONG POSSESSIVE FORMS.

EXERCISE I.

1. Take two cupsful of flour, and one of sugar.
2. He accounted for all monies received by him.
3. There are three Mary's in the class.
4. Eight Henries have sat on the throne of England.
5. I think that her two son-in-laws might support her.
6. He generally forgets to cross his ts or dot his is.
7. You can scarcely tell her 5s from her 3s.
8. Court-martials were held at various points to try the captured insurgents.
9. How many Cantoes have you read?
10. Such crisises may occur in the history of any enterprise.
11. Summons were issued for the chief offenders.
12. These specimens belong to different genuses.
13. The animalculae in water can be seen quite plainly with it.
14. We have opened out several cases of mens' and boys' overalls.
15. Look at the trains of these ladie's dresses.
16. Six month's interest was due on the note.
17. Ten days notice requires to be given in such cases.
18. I saw a sign with " Boat's to hire " on it.
19. For goodness sake don't let him know about it.
20. Virgils similies are mostly borrowed from Homer.

2

ADJECTIVES.

Errors in the use of,

      I.—THE SO-CALLED ARTICLES, *a, an,* and *the.*
      II.—THE DEMONSTRATIVES *these* and *those.*
      III.—COMPARATIVE AND SUPERLATIVE FORMS.

EXERCISE II.

1. What sort of a house does he live in?
2. Such a man does not deserve the name of a gentleman.
3. There must have been more than an hundred of them.
4. Is he an African or an European?
5. The government is a hereditary monarchy.
6. A lion is the emblem of England.
7. She is entitled to the third of the property.
8. I don't like these sort of pens.
9. It isn't safe to trust those kind of people.
10. No man ever had a faithfuller friend.
11. He is the awkwardest looking fellow you ever saw.
12. I place the most entire confidence in his statements.
13. There could not have been less than fifty people in the room.
14. I have nothing farther to say to you at present.
15. The last news is that they are to start on Monday.
16. Give this book to the youngest of the two girls.
17. He answered better than any boy in his class.
18. London has the largest population of any city in the world.
19. The S. has the largest circulation of any other paper in the country.
20. You of all other girls in the class ought to be the last to complain.

PRONOUNS.

WRONG FORMS, OR WRONG USE OF PERSONAL, ADJECTIVE, AND RELATIVE PRONOUNS.

EXERCISE III.

1. Arn't you afraid of his cutting hisself?
2. They ran away and hid theirselves.
3. This is a later edition than your's.
4. Our's is much larger than their's.
5. Pick up them books off the floor.
6. Mr. M. and myself took a walk down to the bank.
7. He has several editions, either of which will serve your purpose.
8. Neither of the three methods is absolutely correct.
9. There is a row of elms on either side of the road.
10. These two boys are always quarrelling with one another.
11. The scholars soon get acquainted with each other.
12. He walked up and down from one end of the room to another.
13. He went about the room, from one to the other, seeking sympathy.
14. I trusted to my horse, who knew the way better than I did.
15. Even newspapers who advertise them are liable to be fined.
16. He is the greatest poet which this century has produced.
17. He remembered the names of most of the authors and books of which we had been speaking.
18. It will take all which he has earned this week.
19. He was the first scholar who succeeded in answering it.
20. I gave it to the boy what brings the milk.

EXERCISE IV.—REVIEW.

1. Don't buy any more of those sort of pencils.
2. Apply to Messrs. C. and D., Barristers and Attornies.
3. These are the only cities who have adopted the system.
4. He brought three hats, neither of which was mine.
5. What kind of a bird is that on the fence ?
6. Did you ever read Bunyans Pilgrims Progress ?
7. Which is the heaviest, her's or mine ?
8. Where did you get them apples ?
9. It was one of the cowardlliest acts I ever heard of.
10. They keep coming in two's and three's.
11. The two criminals soon became suspicious of one another.
12. Of all other places in the world it's the last that I should think of.
13. You can't tell his ns from his us.
14. It presented an unique appearance.
15. One of the negroes sang two soloes at the concert.
16. You never saw a wretcheder looking specimen of humanity.
17. Prove your answer by casting out the 9s.
18. She is a better writer than any scholar in her class.
19. He showed me several, but I did not care for either of them.
20. He sets the hardest papers of any examiner I know.
21. What return do you expect for all which you have done for him ?
22. He would not come any further with us.
23. I gave it to one of the men which were working in the yard.
24. I heard that one of his brother-in-laws had bought the farm.
25. We kept them as mementoes of our six weeks holiday trip.
26. Presently my dog, who had followed me, began to growl.
27. He must have fired not less than five or six shots at it.

28. I met Mrs. C. and himself on their way to church.
29. She doesn't like these kind of pianoes.
30. Many an one would have refused to do it.

VERBS.

I.—THE USE OF THE WRONG AUXILIARY.
II.—WRONG FORMS FOR THE PAST TENSE AND THE PAST
PARTICIPLE.
III.—USING TRANSITIVE VERBS FOR INTRANSITIVE ONES.

EXERCISE V.

1. Can I have the use of your ruler for a little while?
2. They wanted to know if they could not have a holiday.
3. Will I find you at home this evening?
4. Would I be allowed to try the examination?
5. I hope we will be in time to get good seats.
6. He was afraid that we would miss the train.
7. I have resolved that I shall make the attempt.
8. He had little hope that they should accept the offer.
9. I know he done it, for I seen him do it.
10. You have went over that lesson several times.
11. He must have forgot to put the cork in the bottle.
12. He came very near getting his leg broke.
13. He rung the bell twice this morning.
14. The children sung several hymns.
15. They sunk several wells in the neighborhood.
16. The toast was drank with great enthusiasm.
17. He must surely have mistook the house.
18. I think that you might have wrote and told us.
19. You might have chose something more appropriate.
20. He would have froze to death if we had left him.

21. That lesson is tore out of my book.
22. He throwed it over the fence and run for home.
23. He jumped in and swum across.
24. It will be all eat up before you get there.
25. He had began his sermon before they entered.
26. He must have ran all the way home.
27. The passengers all besecched him to return.
28. He said that his feet swole up to a great size.
29. Stung by her reproaches, he went and hung himself.
30. The river had overflown its banks during the night.
31. After he laid down he remembered he had left it laying on the table.
32. You had better go and lay down for a little while.
33. She could not get her bread to raise properly.
34. I wish you would set still while I am copying this.
35. He was forced to fly the country in consequence.

EXERCISE VI.—REVIEW.

1. Which is the furthest north, New York or San Francisco?
2. I would like to hear his opinion of those sort of desks.
3. I seen it laying on your desk a few minutes ago.
4. What sort of a proposition is it?
5. The tug rescued two vessels, who were in distress.
6. It is likely that I will be gone before you return.
7. He must have drank nearly three spoonsful of it.
8. They asked if they could not go at intermission.
9. Several combatants had already fallen on either side.
10. Surely he can't have ate it all already.
11. He offered a prize to any one that would guess the answer.
12. It claims to have the ablest staff of any of its contemporaries.

13. Can't we go when we finish this sum?
14. We have come to the conclusion that we will not be able
    to accept his offer.
15. He looks as if he had laid there all night.
16. The unicorn was probably a kind of a rhinoceros.
17. It was decided that Mr. A., would accompany them to
    the city.
18. The entertainment was a most complete failure.
19. Will we do this one the same way we done the last?
20. It is the likeliest place of all others in town to find him.
21. I was in hopes that we would have a chance to see him
22. He has a better memory than any boy I know of.
23. If I had not broke your stick you would never have ran
    home or began to cry.
24. The same man which left the parcel took it away again.
25. He found that the water had raised several inches.
26. He went about from one door to the other begging.
27. It was the peacefullest meeting they have had for some
    time.
28. He would have went this morning if I hadn't forgot to
    waken him.
29. It is two stories higher than their's.
30. For him through hostile camps I wend my way,
    For him thus prostrate at thy feet I lay.

ADVERBS.

THE USE OF ADJECTIVES FOR ADVERBS, AND ADVERBS FOR ADJECTIVES.

EXERCISE VII.

1. He behaved so bad that I had to suspend him.
2. She seemed real glad to see us.
3. Come quick and see this butterfly.
4. Read it slower, if you please.
5. He acted very different from his brother.
6. He writes plainer now than he once did.
7. You can buy them as cheap here as in Toronto.
8. Walk as quiet as you can.
9. I managed that part of it easy enough.
10. He acted as friendly as if there had never been any quarrel.
11. The children marched quietly and orderly through the hall.
12. He acted very independent about the matter.
13. He scattered the seed quite thick on the ground.
14. He spoke quite decided on that point.
15. The room smelt strong of tobacco.
16. She went to bed and slept sound till morning.
17. They were exceeding glad to see him.
18. Isn't it near finished yet?
19. He ought to dress more suitable to his position.
20. Just as like as not you will meet him on the road.
21. Be careful to sew them on good and strong.
22. They acted very unfriendly towards us.
23. How sweetly these roses smell.
24. How beautifully your garden looks this morning.
25. The order must have sounded harshly to them.

PREPOSITIONS.

THE USE OF THE WRONG PREPOSITION.

EXERCISE VIII.

1. Divide these apples between these three boys.
2. I found it very different to what I expected.
3. Compare your work to his, and you will see the difference.
4. If seemed quite grand in comparison to mine.
5. He let his axe fall in the creek, while crossing.
6. The accident is likely to be attended by serious consequences.
7. She seemed quite overcome by sorrow at the discovery.
8. Is the music accompanied by the words?
9. He was accused with acting unfairly as judge.
10 He was quite ill with typhoid fever at the time.
11. Try to rid yourself from all such prejudices.
12. I hope that he will profit from his experience.
13. I beg to differ from the last speaker.
14. He was very liberal with promises before the election.
15. I did it in compliance to their request.
16. It flew up in the tree before I was ready to fire.
17. The whole room was redolent with the perfume.
18. He refused to conform with the regulations.
19. I did not take notice to what he said.
20. He was rather noted for his fondness of fast horses.
21. She felt the need for some one to advise her.
22. How do you reconcile this statement to your previous one.
23. She had not been accustomed with such treatment.
24. He would be very angry at us if he knew.
25. There was too long an interval between each game.

CONJUNCTIONS.

I.—CONJUNCTIONS WRONGLY USED.

II.—WORDS WRONGLY USED AS CONJUNCTIONS.

EXERCISE IX.

1. I don't know as I can give you his exact words.
2. It could not have got away without somebody untied the halter.
3. Scarcely had he gone to bed than there came a knock at the door.
4. Hardly had he left the room than the prisoner attempted to escape.
5. No sooner had he opened the door when the flames burst forth.
6. Directly he reached home he sent for the doctor.
7. I will start at it immediately they have gone.
8. He took quite a different view than I did.
9. I prefer to wait a few days than to accept an inferior article.
10. Who could do otherwise but accept such an offer?
11. No other course but that was open to him.
12. Nothing else but weeds will grow on it.
13. Why don't you do like I do?
14. It treated him just like a cat would treat a mouse.
15. There is no doubt but what he said so.
16. He gave her a handsome pony, and which cost him fifty pounds.
17. They captured several prisoners but whom they treated very fairly.
18. He found that after paying all expenses that there would be a small sum left.
19. The chances are ten to one but he will forget it.
20. Neither the foreman or his assistant had seen it.

EXERCISE X.—REVIEW.

1. He must have came after we had went home.
2. How will we know which of the two is the best?
3. She was disgusted at him for acting so silly.
4. I cannot explain all the minutia of the process.
5. Their farm lays in a different direction to ours.
6. Your method seems quite simple compared to his.
7. He claims to have answered the most questions of any boy in the class.
8. It seems that he acted wiser than they thought.
9. He fell in the river and was nearly drowned
10. You will scarcely find a more universal blunder.
11. She told them to set up straight so as she could see them all.
12. He wandered about from one street to the other.
13. What is the distance between each telegraph pole?
14. He chose this verse because he thought it would be easiest learned.
15. After a few minutes search they found it laying in a corner.
16. He died very sudden, I am told.
17. He acted just like a boy does when he is telling a lie.
18. I have no doubt but what we will all be benefited by it.
19. Of all other vices covetousness enters deepest into the soul.
20. No other course was left them but to accept his resignation, and which they accordingly did.
21. Mamma, can't we have a party on Saturday?
22. I think you acted very foolish in refusing it.
23. For pity sake do be quiet, girls!
24. It ended in establishing his authority firmer than ever.
25. I will be ten years old next Monday.
26. There is scarcely any one so poor but what can give something.
27. It wasn't Tom that done it, for I seen his hat laying in the hall.

28. The book is illustrated by several fine engravings.
29. He would not go without I promised to pay his expenses.
30. The case is different with city battalions, who are composed mainly of intelligent mechanics and artizans.

EXERCISE XI.—REVIEW.

I.—WHICH OF THE ITALICIZED WORDS IN THE FOLLOWING SENTENCES IS PREFERABLE, AND WHY?

1. It tastes quite *strong* (*strongly*) of cloves.
2. He told them to sit *quiet* (*quietly*) in their seats.
3. I fear that he will pay *dear* (*dearly*) for his rashness.
4. They lived just as *happy* (*happily*) as before.
5. This carriage rides *easy* (*easily*).
6. He felt very *bad* (*badly*) at being beaten.
7. Your piano sounds quite *different* (*differently*) from ours.
8. He stood *firm* (*firmly*) in his place.

II.—DISTINGUISH BETWEEN.

1. The Lord's Day   The Day of the Lord.
2. My sister's photograph. A photograph of my *sister* (*sister's*).
3. The tailor and clothier. The tailor and the clothier.
4. Half a dollar. A half dollar.
5. I found the way *easy* (*easily*).
6. It looks *good* (*well*).
7. She looked *sad* (*sadly*).
8. He turned *quiet* (*quietly*).
9. (*A*) few know of it.
10. She was the greatest *actor* (*actress*) of her day.
11. She has done her sum. She has her sum done.
12. He (*has*) deposited the money in the bank.

III.—GIVE SENTENCES ILLUSTRATING THE CORRECT USE OF THE FOLLOWING.

1. Angry at, with.
2. Compare to, with.
8. Consist of, in.
4. Die of, by.
5. Differ from, with.
6. Divide between, among.
7. Dissapointed of, in.
8. Familiar to, with.
9. Live in, at,
10. Overcome by, with.
11. Reconcile to, with.
12. Taste of, for.

IV.—(a) DISTINGUISH IN MEANING.

1. You will (shall) know the result to-morrow.
2. I will (shall) not be the only one to suffer.
3. Will (shall) he be allowed to withdraw it?
4. Will (shall) you call at the office?
5. He thought she would (should) have another chance.

(b) WHICH OF THE ITALICIZED FORMS IN THE FOLLOWING SHOULD BE USED, AND WHY?

6. *Will (shall)* you be sorry to leave Toronto?
7. He tells me that he *will (shall)* be ten next month.
8. *Will (shall)* I be allowed another trial?
9. He has decided that he *will (shall)* not return it.
10. He offers a prize to whoever *will (shall)* guess it.
11. We *would (should)* be pleased to have you call and see it.
12. *Would (should)* you be surprised to hear of it?
13. I *would (should)* write to him if I knew his address.
14. What *would (should)* we do without you?
15. He promised that it *would (should)* not occur again.

PART II.

ERRORS OF SYNTAX.

CONCORD OR AGREEMENT.

I.—WANT OF AGREEMENT BETWEEN THE VERB AND ITS SUBJECT.

EXERCISE XII.

1. Each of the candidates were allowed another trial.
2. Not one of all those boys were able to answer the question.
3. Nearly every one of the applicants were from this county.
4. Neither of the answers given to it were quite correct.
5. Have either of you seen my pencil?
6. Neither the Mayor nor the Reeve were at the meeting.
7. Either ignorance or carelessness have caused this.
8. Nobody but the speakers and the reporters were allowed on the platform.
9. Nothing but trials and disappointments seem to await me.
10. Economy, as well as industry, are necessary to achieve such a result.
11. The costliness of his arms and apparel were evident at a glance.
12. Efficiency, and not numbers, are what we should aim at.
13. Every door and every window were crowded with spectators.
14. A fine collection of apples were particularly noticeable.
15. Pharaoh, with his whole army, were drowned in the Red Sea.
16. More than one accident has happened in that way.

17. Was you at school the day it happened?
18. It is one of the hardest papers that has ever been given.
19. It may have been one of the men that works in the foundry.
20. To this cause, no doubt, is due most of the failures.
21. What is the mood and tense of the following verbs?
22. Sufficient data has been given to solve it.
23. Thinks I to myself, he will soon see his mistake.
24. Thou art the man that hast done this great wrong.
25. I am a man that have seen something of the world.

II.—The use of the wrong case of the Subject or Predicate Pronoun.

EXERCISE XIII.

1. Her and I are in the same class at school.
2. Henry and him soon began to quarrel.
3. They don't succeed any better than us.
4. She is older than me, but I am nearly as tall as her.
5. It seems that they, as well as us, had mistaken the house.
6. He said that you and me might go if we liked.
7. I gave it to a man whom I thought was the proprietor.
8. Give it to whomsoever seems to need it most.
9. It must have been her that you saw, not me.
10. It wasn't him that gave it to me.
11. It couldn't have been them that we passed.
12. It may have been us that you heard.
13. I should never have imagined it to be he.
14. Whom does he think it could have been?
15. Who do you take me to be?

III.—Appositives in the wrong case.

IV.—Pronouns not Agreeing with their Antecedents.

EXERCISE XIV.

1. Jones, him that won the prize for drawing, has gone to Montreal.
2. Give this book to young Smith, he that is sitting by the window.
3. Not a boy in the class knew their lessons to day.
4. Each of the gentlemen present offered their assistance.
5. Neither of the workmen had brought their tools.
6. Neither the chairman nor the secretary would give their consent.
7. The father, as well as the son, agreed to use their influence.
8. Nobody but a fool would have left their money in such a place.
9. Nearly every one of those present promised their support.
10. Either Mr A. or Mr. B. will, I have no doubt, lend you their copy.
11. Any pupil wishing to dispose of their copy will find a purchaser.
12. If any one wants it let them say so.
13. There may be more than one boy here that can't sign his name.
14. He isn't one of those men that would abandon his principles for office.
15. I must confess that I am a man that can't keep my temper in such cases.

EXERCISE XV.—REVIEW.

1. Which of you boys left your books laying on the desk ?
2. I thought that he acted rather strange this morning.
3. One after another rose and expressed their approval.
4. Who do you suppose he took her to be ?
5. I like it the best of any machine I have seen.
6. How could any person get such an idea into their head ?
7. Can I have it after you are done with it ?
8. There was lots of fun at the meeting last night.
9. The oldest of the two is about as tall as me.
10? Neither of the sisters were at church this morning.
11. Actions speak plainer than words.
12. These two children seem to be very fond of one another.
13. Your own conscience, and not other men's opinions, are to be your guide.
14. Perhaps it wasn't her that you saw.
15. It must belong to one of the prisoners which escaped from the gaol yesterday.
16. He seemed to think that any sort of an excuse would do.
17. I will not be surprised to find that there was more than one in the plot.
18. It is thought to have been him that first suggested it.
19. It is one of the best answers that has yet been given to the question.
20. Nearly every one of the exercises she gave me had mistakes in them.
21. No city in Canada has suffered so much from fires as Quebec.
22. Of that large collection there remains but a few imperfect specimens
23. We will all be anxious to learn the result.
24. He could not account for all the phenomena that was witnessed.
25. Whom did you say it was that gave it to you.
26. It seems that Mary and her went to school together.
27. I read it slow enough for any one to follow me.

28. The man whom we thought was him proved to be an entire stranger.
29. The moral is that perseverance, coupled with patience and prudence, are sufficient to achieve such results.
30. It is one of the words that doubles the *l* before another syllable.

V.—WRONG TENSES OR MOODS.

EXERCISE XVI.

1. I intended to have written it on Saturday.
2. I expected to have heard from him before this.
3. I was in hopes to have finished it before you came.
4. I meant to have told you about it this morning.
5. I found it harder than I thought it would have been.
6. If I had known in time I might have arranged to have gone with you.
7. I don't see that he has done any more than it was his duty to have done.
8. He has formerly been a resident of the town.
9. It is more than a year since he has visited the school.
10. I have written to him so that he might be ready for us.
11. The fellow scarcely seemed to know that two and two made four.
12 How far did you say it was from Toronto to Montreal?
13. If it was not for that I would go with you.
14. If it is fine to-morrow I may take you for a walk.
15. Take care that he does not find you at this.
16. Go and see if the office be open yet.
17. Clerk wanted   It is indispensable that he write a good hand and has some knowledge of book-keeping.
18. If you would take the trouble to look you will see it.
19. If one went unto them from the dead they will repent.
20. You need not have taken so much trouble.

VI.—THE COUPLING OF DISSIMILAR FORMS OR CONSTRUCTIONS.

EXERCISE XVII.

1. To do without these things is better than going into debt for them.
2. Ere you mark another's sin,
   Bid thy own conscience look within.
3. I always have and always will uphold that view.
4. Has the committee given in their report yet?
5. The committee who drafted the report was composed of the following members.
6. Here is the book that you lent me, and which I forgot to return yesterday.
7. Persons that read the report, and who do not know him, might think so.
8. He is a man of whom I have often heard, but I have never seen him.
9. I dare say she is as old, if not older, than you.
10. He was a better scholar, but not so good a speaker, as his friend.
11. This stuff is coarser and in every way inferior to the other.
12. Doth he not leave the ninety and nine and goeth into the wilderness?
13. Did you not promise to help me, and even offered to bring your team?
14. Will Mr. H. please excuse John's absence, and oblige, yours truly, A. B.
15. Miss C.'s compliments to Mr. S., and will feel greatly obliged if you will inform me whether, &c.
16. The undersigned has received instructions from the Government Inspector, who has just visited my office, to enforce the regulations.
17. Not having any money, and as I knew no one in the village, I was forced to continue my journey.
18. In this way they learn to steal and many other vices.
19. He promised to find out and that he would send us word.
20. I blame him for having led us here and then leaving us.

EXERCISE XVIII.—REVIEW.

1. If I was him I would be ashamed to go there again.
2. By the term fossils is meant the petrified remains of animals and plants.
3. We sorrow not as them that have no hope.
4. Hardly had she entered the car than she discovered her loss.
5. I meant to have given you several of those sort of questions.
6. Hers is one of those impulsive natures that longs for a confidant.
7. I have frequently been asked what we teachers did at our meetings.
8. I mean Noah Webster, he that wrote the dictionary.
9. I thought I would have been able to have finished it to-night.
10. The mob appears to have come to their senses at last.
11. He speaks to every one as friendly as if they were his relations.
12. It will do as good, if not better work, than any machine in the market.
13. A careful examination of all these facts lead to the belief.
14. As I never saw one before I was greatly surprised.
15. One needs to have all their senses about them at such a time.
16. It must have been very difficult to have kept it secret so long.
17. A rhombus is a four-sided figure whose sides are equal, but its angles are not right angles.
18. Thy thrilling trump had roused the land.
    When fraud or danger were at hand.
19. I thought I would have died laughing at his ridiculous appearance.
20. His second proposal was quite different and superior to the first.
21. How long is it since you have heard from your brother ?

22. I dare say we will find that more than one has had a hand in it.

23. The subscriber has just received a large stock of fresh groceries at his new store on B. st., where I will be happy to wait upon my customers.

24. The prize is to be given to whomsoever will answer the most questions correctly.

25. If he was at home he would give us any quantity of it.

26. These funds will be available for meeting such expences, and to enable the committee to carry out the scheme properly.

27. It is recommended that he shall be one of the masters of the school, and who shall reside on the premises.

28. It is one of the hardest papers that has ever been given and I will not be surprised if nearly every one of the candidates fail on it.

29. Was it him that argued that the earth was flat.

30. These duties should be performed by an officer whose duties should be defined by the committee, and his salary paid by the Board.

———

EXERCISE XIX.—REVIEW.

I.—WHICH OF THE ITALICIZED VERB FORMS IN THE FOLLOW-
ING SENTENCES WOULD YOU PREFER, AND WHY?

1. It is I that *is* (*am*) to blame.

2. Three times two *is* (*are*) six.

3. The ebb and flow of the tide *was* (*were*) explained by Newton.

4. More than a century and a half *has* (*have*) elapsed since that.

5. About fifty feet of the bridge *was* (*were*) swept away by the freshet.

6. Ph in such words *has* (*have*) the sound of f.

7. Two and two *makes* (*make*) four.

8. Enough labour and money *has* (*have*) been spent on it already.

9. To invent calumnies, and to spread suspicion, *requires* (*require*) neither labour nor courage.

10. To admit the existence of such a God, and then to refuse to worship him, *is* (*are*) surely inconsistent.

II.—How would you justify the use of the Singular Verb in the following sentences?

1. When 9 *is* subtracted from 17 what *is* left?

2. The spectator and historian of the battle *tells* us.

3. Two thousand dollars *was* scarcely sufficient to pay all the expences.

4. There *was* racing and chasing on Cannobie Lea.

5. A block and tackle *was* made use of in raising it.

6. Wherein *doth* sit the dread and fear of kings.

7. For thine *is* the kingdom, and the power, and the glory.

8. Happiness, honor, nay life itself, *is* sacrified in pursuit of it.

9. Early to bed, and early to rise,
   Makes a man healthy, wealthy, and wise.

10. Every chapter, and indeed every page, *furnishes* proof of this.

11. For a laggard in love, and a dastard in war,
    Was to wed the fair Ellen of young Lochinvar.

12. It must be one of our opponents that *has* done this.

GOVERNMENT.

I.—USING THE NOMINATIVE CASE AFTER TRANSITIVE VERBS AND PREPOSITIONS.

II.—USING PREPOSITIONS AFTER TRANSITIVE VERBS.

EXERCISE XX.

1. Let you and I go for a pailful of water.
2. I offered to let Mary and she divide it equally.
3. I cannot permit you and he to sit together any longer.
4. You may appoint whoever you like.
5. Who were you talking to just now?
6. Who did you expect to see?
7. Can't you remember who you got it from?
8. Between you and I it looks rather suspicious.
9. He left word for John and I to call on our way home.
10. Girls like you and she ought to be ashamed to act so.
11. I mentioned it to those whom I met, and she among the rest.
12. There seems to be nobody here but you and I.
13. All the girls had gone except her and I.
14. He refused to accept of any remuneration for his services.
15. I will not allow of such conduct in this room.
16. I don't recollect of any similar instance.
17. I remember of hearing him make the statement.
18. He will not permit of any interruption.
19. He shall not want for money while I have any.
20. Who was that lady standing near you and I?

III.—The Neglect or Misuse of the Possessive Case.

EXERCISE XXI.

1. There is no use in me trying the examination
2. Is there any prospect of the Council passing such a by-law ?
3. A dog and a cat's head are differently shaped.
4. Whose dictionary do you prefer? Webster, or Worcester ?
5. He lived in Charles II.'s reign.
6. It is neither the purser nor the steward's duty.
7. For Herodias' sake, his brother Philip's wife.
8. That is my brother James's wife's youngest sister.

EXERCISE XXII.—REVIEW.

1. I did not succeed quite so well as I wished to have done.
2. I don't know as the exact cost is known yet.
3. You are not the first boy that have made that mistake.
4. The blow will fall heavier on this community than on most others.
5. At the head of the party was Fox and Lord Grey.
6. Each of the candidates pledged themselves to abide by his decision.
7. That remark must have been intended for you and I.
8. It is one of the worst cases that has come under my notice.
9. If I was her I would be afraid of him finding out who done it.
10. He professed to believe that the soul perished with the body.
11. He refused to comply to the demands of the Board.
12. Neither by you or he was it seemingly regarded as necessary.
13. The committee which was appointed to consider the matter have brought in a long report.

14. I don't see but what you have as good a right to it as her.
15. I would have liked very much to have had a talk with him.
16. When a person makes such a mistake they generally try to conceal it.
17. The "Elegy" is one of the few poems that is not injured by constant repetition.
18. He knows as much, if not more Greek than most graduates.
19. Neither of us had any mistakes in our exercises.
20. I would probably have gone independent of his offer.
21. It is the most perfect specimen which I have seen for a long time.
22. I don't care who I work for, as long as I get my pay.
23. Neither will they be persuaded though one rose from the dead.
24. It, as well as several of the others, seem to have been carelessly done.
25. I cannot excuse those whose business it was to have attended to it.
26. It makes no difference whom you thought it was.
27. What will be the consequences if the examination papers were made easier, or more mechanical?
28. The amount of all these alterations and additions are so great as to make it look like a new book.
29. Telegraph me directly you reach Buffalo.
40. I thought I spoke plain enough on that point yesterday.

3

POSITION.

THE MISPLACEMENT OF CONJUNCTIONS, ADVERBS, ADVERBIAL PHRASES, AND RELATIVE CLAUSES.

EXERCISE XXIII.

1. He both taught them to read and to write.
2. He neither answered my letter nor my card.
3. He was not competent either to teach classics or mathematics.
4. Such a task would be alike barren of instruction and amusement.
5. It will not merely interest the children, but also the parents.
6. You are not only mistaken in your inferences, but also in your facts.
7. I have only received one letter from her since she left.
8. He only rents the store, not the house.
9. His dexterity almost appeared miraculous.
10. He must have wanted to see them very much.
11. I forgot to sign my name to a letter once.
12. I fear that it will be necessary to entirely remodel it.
13. I beg to respectfully recommend its adoption.
14. I scarcely ever remember hearing one that I liked better.
15. Everybody thought that it was destined to be a great city, twenty years ago.
16. He came very near being struck more than once during the row.
17. They followed his ascent, step by step, through telescopes.
18. He rose speedily in his employer's estimation, who very much respected him.
19. He is unworthy of the confidence of a fellow being that disregards the laws of his Maker.
20. Bosworth was the last battle of the wars of the Roses in which Richard the Third was slain.

EXERCISE XXIV.—REVIEW.

1. He invented some sort of a machine for the purpose.
2. The schools are very different now to what they were then.
3. That was the Mayor, as well as the Reeve's opinion.
4. Neither of the books that you seen laying on the floor were mine.
5. It was his duty to have corrected the error at once.
6. At least ten thousand dollars worth of property were destroyed by the fire.
7. It is as cold, if not colder, than any day this winter.
8. It may have been Mr. A. and not her that done it.
9. The Board has appointed Mr. M. to audit their accounts.
10. Who do you think Mary and her met on their way home.
11. If I was to remove this weight what would happen?
12. I have been told that he has visited them quite recently.
13. He acknowledged that he had intended to have used it.
14. Shakespeare is more true to nature than any writer I know of.
15. Every day, and in fact every hour, bring their changes.
16. No people was ever more fiercely assailed by persecution than those of this country.
17. The junior classes are, if not better, at least as well taught as the senior ones.
18. The family with whom she has been boarding has decided to return to Michigan.
19. Will either of you girls lend this boy your slate?
20. His long experience, joined to his natural aptitude for teaching, enable him to accomplish this.
21. Nobody but you and I know where to find them.
22. You must learn to carefully distinguish between these two forms.
23. He was not only noted for his theoretical knowledge, but also for his practical skill.
24. Neither he or his wife seem to care what sort of an example they set their children.
25. The meaning of words, phrases, and sentences are taken up with the class before reading the lesson.

26. I have very little hope of him passing the examination.
27. You should not accept of such an excuse.
28. At that time Mexico was both more populous and more civilized than any country in America.
29. The same wind detained the king's fleet in their station at Harwich.
30. It affords the opportunity of considering whether his purpose in establishing the school, and which has so far remained unfulfilled, cannot now be carried out.

MISCELLANEOUS SYNTACTICAL ERRORS.

I. DOUBLE NEGATIVES.—II. ELLIPSIS.—III. PLEONASM.

EXERCISE XXV.

1. Neither you nor nobody else ever saw me do it.
2. Henceforth I cannot nor will not make any allowance in such cases.
3. The Council has not now, nor never had the power to pass such a by-law.
4. He didn't leave any here, I don't think.
5. He isn't likely to come by this train, I don't suppose.
6. There wasn't hardly anybody there that I knew.
7. No two teachers could hardly differ more in style.
8. The past and present condition of Greece are very different.
9. The determining the boundary line is the most important matter.
10. For sale, a Dictionary and Atlas, both nearly new.
11. There isn't one that can't read, and few that can't write.
12. The man who was left in charge of it, and attends to it, is beginning to wonder.
13. He has got a good deal more to do this term.
14. He will be here in the latter end of next week.
15. He was a child of ten years old at the time.
16. His two sisters were both at the meeting.

17. The funeral will take place at three p.m. to-morrow afternoon.
18. She met in with them on her way home.
19. There are generally a good many go to them.
20. His mother was a poor widow woman.
21. Lend me the loan of your ruler for a little while.
22. I know not from whence he came, or where he went to.
23. Whenever I see her she always asks about you.
24. Before you go you must first finish your exercise.
25. I came as fast as ever I could.
26. It is a good plan to adopt with new beginners.
27. I never saw the man before in my life.
28. He did it equally as well as his friends.
29. I have spoilt this envelope, bring me another one.
30. It must be ten years ago since he left home.

COMMON IMPROPRIETIES AND VULGARISMS.

EXERCISE XXVI.

1. She looked kind of surprised when she found you here.
2. I sort of thought you would come to-night.
3. I'm just after writing to him for some more.
4. He hadn't ought to have told her about it.
5. She would not stay, being as how she was all alone.
6. He told me that he used to could do that.
7. He would have gone home if I had not have stopped him.
8. I see them most every day.
9. He was some better when we left him this morning.
10. He came very near being drownded.
11. The dog attackted him on the street.
12. He left home unbeknown to his parents.
13. The doctor wasn't to home when I called.

14. This here answer aint correct.
15. That there boy don't seem to be attending.
16. Tell that hind boy to sit down.
17. Whatever did you do that for.
18. I wanted to go but couldn't get.
19. She lives quite a long ways from the school.
20. He walked quite a piece of the road with us?
21. Where are you stopping at present?
22. I wont believe him again.
23. I aint got that answer.
24. It isn't quite that bad.
25. Are you not done your sums yet?
26. Apples will not be so plenty th's fall.
27. The house is plenty large enough for them.
28. I wish you would learn me how to do it.
29. I expect he must have gone home.
30. He is generally allowed to keep the best hotel in town.
31. Will you loan me your knife for a few minutes?
32. He seldom or ever visits the school now.
33. I never remember hearing him speak of it.
34. Try and remember to shut the door after you.
35. He knows more than you think for.
36. He went up-stairs for to get some paper.
37. Leave me be, I tell you.
38. He woudn't have known if you hadn't of told him.
39. I wish I had a known that sooner.
40. He gave her the watch in a present.
41. He ran the cart again the window.
42. Some days his conduct is very aggravating.
43. We saw some awfully nice cards at S's.
44. He seems to have a mighty poor opinion of their ma-chines.
45. I did know but I disremember it just now.
46. A finite verb must agree with its nominative in number and person.

47. She was quite mad at me for telling him.
48. He didn't seem overly anxious to go.
49. I found a couple of misspelled words in your exercise.
50. He'll get himself into a fix some day, if he isn't careful.

EXERCISE XXVII.—REVIEW.

1. Was it a man or a woman's voice that we heard?
2. In what State did you say Chicago was?
3. Such a course is likely to be attended by much danger.
4. No one in England knew what tea was two hundred years ago.
5. These girls will neither listen, nor let nobody else listen.
6. Neither you or I are in the wrong.
7. You will not find him to home this morning, I don't think.
8. There is need of institutions like U. C. College ought to be.
9. It was a place of which we had heard much, but we had never visited it.
10. Any boy with any sense in their head would have known the difference.
11. Men are in the plural number because they mean several.
12. Wanted a nurse and housemaid, who must both have good refer u es.
13. His method of solving it was quite different to mine.
14. It seems to me that you have weakened instead of strengthened your ca-e.
15. He is only fitted to govern others who can govern himself.
16. Neither Paine nor Voltaire were able to advance any new objections.
17. The party whom he had invited was both numerous and select.

18. He never has and probably never will forgive me for deceiving him.
19. Its last statements are quite as reckless, and even more malicious than its former ones.
20. He was not only accused of theft, but also of murder.
21. All males are of the masculine gender, and females of the feminine.
22. If he don't come be sure and let me know.
23. I would have been there by this time if you hadn't have delayed me.
24. Nothing but balls and parties seem to have any interest for her.
25. You can go as soon as you are done your exercise.
26. There is over one hundred buildings gone up since last spring.
27. What is to prevent him finding out who done it?
28. Hoping that I will hear from you soon believe me, yours truly, A. B.
29. Twenty-four hours notice are usually given in such cases.
30. I felt kind of frightened at first.
31. He said it was her that begun it.
32. When a nation forms a government it is power, not wisdom, which they place in the hands of that government.
33. You wasn't paying attention to the explanation, I don't think.
34. The committee is to meet at 10 a. m. on Wednesday forenoon.
35. Nobody but the doctor and the nurse are allowed to see him.
36. Wont he be surprised to find that we aint going?
37. Each of you boys have got as much as you can carry.
38. Has the jury brought in their verdict yet?
39. Try and remember where you left it laying.
40. Many of our best scholars lack that knowledge of business affairs which are so essential to success.

EXERCISE XXVIII.—REVIEW.

I.—JUSTIFY, OR CORRECT (GIVING REASONS) THE FORM OF THE
ITALICIZED WORDS IN THE FOLLOWING SENTENCES.

1. I am a plain blunt man that *love my* friend.
2. It is you and not your brother that *deserves* to be blamed.
3. And many a holy text around she strews,
   That *teach* the rustic moralist to die.
4. My robe and my integrity to heaven *is* all I dare now
   call mine own.
5. Nine-tenths of all that misery is caused by idleness.
6.   A generous troop *appears*
   Who *spread their* bucklers and *advance their* spears.
7. There *is* a tribe in these mountains who *are* fairer colored
   and more intelligent than the rest of the natives.
8. Mathematics *is* regarded as of more importance than
   English.
9. His marks in the different subjects were as *follows*.
10. I have ventured *this* many summers in a sea of glory.
11. There is no doubt of its being *she*.
12. *Previous* to retiring he left orders to be called early.

II.—DISTINGUISH IN MEANING BETWEEN,

1. Much depends on the teacher (teacher's) correcting the
   papers.
2. Just think of him (his) being engaged in such work.
3. He was an abler statesman than (a) soldier.
4. She sings as well as (she) plays.
5. One of the causes that has (have) not been mentioned is
   the following.
6. I am the man that gives (give) out the tickets.
7. He was careful to work out (in working out) the question for them.
8. He expressed the pleasure he felt in hearing the (in the
   hearing of the) philosopher.
9. If I have (had) (had had) the book I, &c.
10. If he did it he would (should) be punished.
11. If he was (were) present what should I do?
12. I remember an anecdote of the doctor (doctor's) which
    may interest you.

MISCELLANEOUS GRAMMATICAL ERRORS.

EXERCISE XXIX.—REVIEW.

1. It wasn't her that done it, I don't think.
2. Which is the cheapest, to go by Toronto, or by Hamilton?
3. There is no two of them exactly alike.
4. But for you and I he would have been drownded.
5. He would have laid there all night, if we had not have wakened him.
6. Can I leave my seat for a few minutes?
7. Is there any one in the class that don't understand it?
8. Who did you give the parcel to?
9. Her and I can carry it easy enough.
10. If any pupil has seen anything of it I will be glad if they will let me know.
11. Each candidate must provide their own stationery.
12. How will I know who to give it to.
13. We don't want no loafers here.
14. There is surely some other places of importance.
15. Wasn't you awfully glad to get home?
16. Whom did he say had been appointed secretary?
17. It must be nearly ten years since I have been in Toronto.
18. He don't seem to bowl as good as he used to.
19. He is just as honest, if not more so, than any of his neighbors.
20. Two teaspoonsful of the mixture, dissolved in a glass of water, and drank during effervescence, makes a cooling drink.
21. I have not heard of anybody but the Smith's that are invited.
22. It was so dark that I couldn't see the horses, hardly.
23. They seem to me to be nearly dressed alike.
24. What did he say the name of this station was?
25. There is no chance of him passing without he works harder.

26. It aint likely that I will be able to finish it to-day.
27. Who do you think we met this morning ?
28. What have you got in your hand ?
29. I meant to have written it this morning.
30. Have either of you a copy of the questions that was given at last examination ?
31. I would have done it as cheap as him if you had asked me.
32. You will seldom or ever find him to home in the evening.
33. Probably more than one teacher present has met with such cases.
34. That place aint marked on the map, I don't think.
35. I think it must be some sort of a fever.
36. Nobody but you and she were in the room since.
37. I don't see that he either has or can gain anything by it.
38. Where would we find any one willing to go to so much trouble ?
39. He asked me if he could not have the use of it for a few days.
40. How long is it since you have heard from your brother ?
41. It is one of the most interesting articles that has appeared in the " Monthly."
42. I sold them to Johnson, he that has a shop on W. St.
43. Neither Holmes nor Thompson were class-mates of mine.
44. Let every one attend to their own slate
45. He thinks that what he don't know aint worth knowing.
46. I have heard nothing of it, neither from him or his friends.
47. I prefer to wait for him than to go alone.
48. You can't deny but what you received notice.
49. He seemed to have every confidence of his ability to finish it.
50. That needn't make any difference between old friends like you and I.
51. If you had been working all morning like we have you would be glad to rest.
52. Nobody but you and I seem to know about it.
53. Sixteen multiplied by six equals to what ?

54. There could not have been a more unanimous meeting.
55. I had a better opinion of you than to have supposed that you would do such a thing.
56. Little more but the names of the authors and their works are given in the notes.
57. It isn't one of the words that adds *es* in the plural.
58. Neither the Old or New Testament contain any such verse.
59. I will have to go alone without he changes his mind.
60. Are you not near done your exercise yet?
61. I don't hardly think he will come to night.
62. Would there be any use in us going to see him about it?
63. Her and I agreed to write to one another every week.
64. A large quantity of military stores and provisions were found in the fort.
65. Who was Cortez sent out by?
66. If any person is not satisfied with the pictures I will refund them their money.
67. I'm just after explaining to the class how to work those sort of questions.
68. Wasn't you at school the day it was broke?
69. We can't wait no longer for them boys.
70. Boys like you and he ought to be ashamed to behave so bad in church.
71. Hold on, Tom! Here comes Smith and two or three other fellows.
72. This letter is from my cousin Annie, she that you met here last summer.
73. See that none are admitted whom you think will not be true to the cause.
74. It is very likely that there was more than one concerned in it.
75. Such prices are only paid in times of great scarcity.
76. He spoke so slow and distinct that I caught every word·
77. Neither Selden nor Bacon were graduates of a University.
78. I kind of thought he might have taken it.
79. If you had went home and asked her perhaps she would have let you come with Jane and I.

80. There isn't any complements, I don't think.
81. Every intelligent mechanic ought to use their influence on his behalf.
82. You never have, and I trust you never will, meet with such a trial.
83. There is no doubt but what he expected to have been first.
84. I told him he could stop at home this afternoon if he liked.
85. But, after all, these are nothing when compared to the advantages it offers.
86. She couldn't answer a single question, scarcely.
87. I wont allow of any interference with my authority.
88. If I was in his place I would be glad to get rid of it.
89. I think that he lived in George III's reign.
90. I look on it as one of the most feasible schemes that has been proposed.
91. She had forgot to tell him that the flour was near done.
92. There aint a book in the library, hardly, but what he has read.
93. Who does he think the association is likely to appoint as their agent here?
94. I was in hopes to have seen you at the party, last night.
95. I am sorry that I haven't got anything better to offer you.
96. Is there anyone in the class that don't understand how to fill up their form?
97. Be sure and let me know if the water raises any higher.
98. My prices will be found as low, if not lower, than can be found elsewhere.
99. My stock is more complete than ever, and customers may rest assured at getting bargains.
100. In her name has been committed some of the vilest crimes which stain the page of history.
101. You can take any that you can find laying on the counter.
102. The spirit, and not the letter of the law are what we ought to look at.

103. It is possible that you may never have such another chance.
104. Be careful in distinguishing between these two words.
105. Mr. H. is one of those who won scholarships but was refused payment.
106. More than one outbreak of typhoid fever has been due to such a state of affairs.
107. It wasn't me that done it ; it was that there boy.
108. This cake tastes quite nicely, after all, don't it ?
109. I can't understand how any one can keep their temper.
110. He evidently didn't know what it was to be afraid.
111. He told us there was two principal propositions in the sentence.
112. He said he would give it to whomsoever would solve the equation first.
113. Suppose that he was to come in and find you acting so disorderly.
114. He had no other course open to him, but to resign, and which he accordingly did.
115. He hasn't gone and ain't likely to.
116. They will be interested when the nature of a syllogism or the fallacy of a proposition are explained to them.
117. In such matters profusion as well as parsimony are to be avoided.
118. The rising and falling inflection require to be carefully distinguished.
119. No one would write a book unless he thinks it will be read.
120. She surely don't expect me to tell who I got it from.
121. His machine works quite different to what I expected.
122. Are either of these places marked on the map ?
123. He may even succeed to make out the sense of the passage.
124. I doubt if there is more than one girl in the class that can spell it correctly.
125. It is said to be homogeneous when the sum of the indices are the same.
126. The inscription gave the name and age of the deceased, merely.

127. I have lost the game, though it seemed to me as if I should have won it.

128. If for $1 I can buy 8 lbs. of raisins, how much can I buy for $5.

129. You have got no right to open it without permission.

130. Mrs. A.'s compliments to Mr. B., and would like if you would be kind enough to send me a list of the books required.

131. When one tries their hand at predicting it is best not to be too definite.

132. Wanted, a short-hand writer, by a legal firm, who can also engross well.

133. It is one of the greatest misfortunes that has or can happen to the town.

134. He was a man whom I greatly respected, but I never really liked him.

135. Is it ignorance or carelessness that are the cause of him failing so often.

136. Was it her that was talking so loud in the next room ?

137. You will never succeed to pass the examination without you are more careful.

138. He told me that you had gone to the city and wasn't to be back till Wednesday.

139. He has no farther need for it, and neither have I.

140. What avails all these advantages if he will not profit from them.

141. Each of us could furnish instances from our own experience.

142. I know of no one better fitted for it, or so likely to give satisfaction as Mr. M.

143. The committee trusts that the citizens will co-operate heartily with them in making the entertainment a success.

144. He hasn't a bit of strength, no more than an infant.

145. He seemed to thoroughly understand the subject.

146. It will cure catarrh quicker than any remedy offered to the public.

147. If it wasn't for the newspapers we would know very little of what is going on around us.

148. Neither my brother nor I were able to endure it any longer.

149. The arranging the programme will take some time.

150. Had I known sooner I would have been able to have made arrangements for him to have stopped with us.

151. Tobacco is derived from the island of Tobago, from which it was first brought.

152. A few inches more or less in a lady's height makes a great difference.

153. You must speak plainer if you wish to be understood.

154. Unless a teacher feels that he or she has a divine mission in the work, they are not likely to succeed.

155. There is a great difference between the present and the past condition of the school.

156. Winter in our temperate climate exhibits very few phenomena in comparison to what is visible in the arctic regions.

157. He said that he should like that the matter would be definitely settled.

158. If not larger, it certainly is quite as large as the specimen which you showed us yesterday.

159. No two positions in life could hardly be more opposite.

160. I don't suppose there was any one in the room but what suspected something.

161. Every tree and every shrub glittered in the sunlight as if they were covered with diamonds.

162. As I never saw a play before, it proved very interesting.

163. Unfortunately he neither knows the name or the residence of the owner.

164. A gentleman living on West St., and who is a frequent visitor in our office handed it to us.

165. 'Tis thine to command, mine to obey, let me know therefore what your orders are.

166. It had been his intention, I believe, to have received us with considerable ceremony.

167. Any who has seen it will admit that we have not, and, indeed, can not do it justice.

168. I see why you do that, quite clearly, but I don't understand the next step.

169. I indeed prefer a man without money than money without a man.
170. The derivation of the word, as well as the usage of our best writers, are in favour of this view.
171. There have been three famous talkers in England, either of whom would serve as an illustration.
172. He has come a long ways expressly for to try the examination.
173. If he was to find out that it was her wrote it he would be very angry.
174. Yet no sooner does morning dawn but the strange enchantment vanishes.
175. I was taken up too much with the thoughts to notice the language with which they were clothed.
176. Every one of the witnesses gave it as their opinion that neither the captain or the mate were to blame for the accident.
177. There is also a council who, though itself irresponsible, governs the educational interests of the Province.
178. He was a man who, though I did not like him, I could not help respecting.
179. We will find that all the most common and useful words, as well as the greater part of the grammar, is native.
180. You can scarcely find a more universal blunder.
181. There are occasions in the life of nearly every one when they cannot find words to adequately express their feelings.
182. A proper dipthong is when both vowels are sounded.
183. It contains a great deal that is useful, and which may be turned to good account.
184. The committee pays the town authorities a high tribute for the courtesy and attention which was shown them during their visit.
185. I aint sure which of the two is the largest.
186. More than one of the candidates seemed anxious to show off his knowledge.
187. To test that I would need to have given the class a written examination.

188. A hasty perusal of this strange production might not show you that it was a poem.

189. The greatest number of candidates came up to that examination of any former year.

190. The crown of England can only be worn by a Protestant.

191. If it wasn't for you and she, and two or three more, I would leave.

192. Emphasis is the laying a greater stress on some words than on others.

193. He struck me as I was jumping onto the sleigh.

194. The court has taken a different view than did the public, and have awarded him a considerable sum.

195. He has just issued his thousandth and first volume.

196. I have very little doubt but what you might find some of them laying around yet, if you would take the trouble to look for them.

197. He looks on it as one of the most admirable military performances that has taken place in modern times.

198. The manufacture of them has now arrived to immense proportions.

199. Neither the power to issue a license, nor the power to regulate the traffic were questions before the court.

200. No professional man, no business man, in fact no man of sense would risk their reputation by supporting such a scheme.

201. We are convinced that were the question brought before the Privy Council it will be found that these powers belong to the Local Legislatures.

202. If I succeed to discharge the duties devolving on me, satisfactorily, it will be because, &c.

203. There are generally a good many go from mere curiosity.

204. He is one of the few who can be depended on to keep his presence of mind on such occasions.

205. Egypt would scarcely have been able to have secured her independence by her own efforts.

206. Color-blindness is so common in some countries that nearly one in every twenty of the inhabitants suffer from it.

207. I know of no method that will accomplish this so effectually, or at less expense than that you have suggested.

208. Like Shakespeare his genius is sublime, and his imagination unbounded.

209. Though her disposition was quite different and superior to his, many causes contributed to render her less popular than him.

210. A. and B. beg to announce that they have commenced business in the above store. Having purchased our stock at close prices we are prepared to offer bargains.

211. After the jury was in the box he wanted to challenge several of them whom he said had a prejudice against his client.

212. The captain admitted that he had had several of his crew died with yellow fever.

213. What is the reason that our language is less refined than those of Italy and France ?

214. At the expiration of the time every one must read what they have written.

215. Short as this gospel is it tells us many things not contained in either of the other three.

216. They supposing him to have been in the company went a day's journey.

217. The future of England depends on each generation showing the same courage, wisdom and moderation as was shown by those who made her what she is.

213. Resolved :—That this society desires to record its conviction that by the removal of C. D. we have lost one of our most active and useful members.

219. Michigan and New Hampshire are the only States electing gubernatorial candidates who have declared for the Republicans.

220. The new hotel belonging to Mr. C., and which was only recently opened to the public, was burned last night.

221. The indebtedness of the English language to the Greek, Latin, and French, is disclosed on every page.

222. One night last week the house of D. W. of this town was entered by a burglar which for cool audacity is seldom beaten.

223. The gentleman must remember that the road was not built simply that he may enjoy a large salary as Managing Director.

224. The Prime Minister with the Chancellor of the Exchequer were admitted to her presence.

225. It is stronger and every way superior to the other one.

226. He said it was a great misfortune that men of letters seldom looked on the practical side of such matters.

227. Personification is when we ascribe life or action to inanimate objects.

228. Nearly every one of the teachers present gave it as their opinion that there was more than one way of interpreting the question, and that consequently neither of the three answers were absolutely wrong.

229. It is much to be regretted that they should, as they have, elected him for their representative.

230. Mrs. A's compliments to Mrs. B., and begs to state that Mary C. lived with me nearly a year, and that I found her capable and honest.

231. He said that he had heard nothing, and did not expect to, before Saturday.

232. His reputation is equal to any writer in the Province.

233. He appeared to clearly understand the various steps of the process.

234. I am one of those people who cannot describe what I have not seen.

235. Did you not agree to sell it to me for $20, and offered to wait three months for your pay?

236. If we were to examine them under a microscope we would find that not one of all these crystals were alike.

237. It is no use in us reasoning any longer with him.

238. In place of the old list I have prepared another, and which I think will be found more useful.

239. He had made so many alterations and additions to the plan that I scarcely recognized it.

240. The King said if he did he would cut off every Frenchman's head that was in his kingdom.

241. At this time the Board of Agriculture was employed in completing their valuable series of county reports.

242. A rapid increase in the number of schools and of the pupils attending them are not at present to be expected.

243. Parties wishing a selection should telegraph, as the goods will not remain long in stock, in order to prevent disappointment.

244. The House of Commons, which represented the middle classes, were apparently afraid, &c.

245. It is surely preferable to die the death of a patriot than to live the life of a slave.

246. If thou bring thy gift to the altar, and there rememberest, &c.

247. Irving and Macaulay's style are very different.

248. Presently I came to a bog into which I knew if I strayed I would never emerge unaided.

249. Now is the time to raise our school into such a state of efficiency that will enable it to prepare pupils for the various Universities.

250. These passages will confirm what I say, and which has only to be stated to be acknowledged by any Bible student.

251. No subject has engaged the time and attention of teachers so much, or been more pressed upon them by parents than reading.

252. This hypothesis, as well as that previously referred to, merely prove the hallucination of the authors.

253. It may be employed to strengthen the impression which we intend that any object should make.

254. If he was wise he would have contented himself to follow their advice.

255. It appears that no one is exempt from serving on a coroner's jury, and may be fined for non-attendance.

256. To-morrow being the last day of the Regatta, and on which takes place the races of the Rowing Club, will doubtless attract a large crowd.

257. The last hitch in this celebrated case appears to be the most absurd of all its predecessors.

258. I regret that some of our number have been led astray, and fallen back into their old habits.

259. As much, and, indeed, sometimes greater evil, is caused
by neglect of duty than by mal-performance of it.

260. The party, though disgraced by the corruption of its
leaders, made a strong effort to regain their former
ascendency.

261. Thou great first cause ! least understood,
Who all my sense confined !

262. Christian and Moor in death promiscuous lay,
Each where they fell.

263. Nor grew it white in a single night,
As other men's have done.

264. Some who the depths of eloquence have found,
In that unnavigable stream were drowned.

265. 'Twas Love's mistake, who fancied what it feared.

266. Just to thy word, in every thought sincere,
Who knew no wish but what the world might hear.

267. Friend to my life, which did you not prolong,
The world had wanted many an idle song.

268. Who art thou ? Speak ! that on designs unknown,
While others sleep, thus range the camps alone.

269. Did ever Proteus, Merlin, or any witch,
Transform themselves so strangely as the rich ?

270. Danger, long travel, want, or woe,
Soon change the form that best we know.

271. O fairest flower ! no sooner blown but blasted !

272. Thou who didst call the Furies from th' abyss,
And round Orestes bade them howl and hiss.

273. Give us the secrets of this Pagan hell,
Where ghost with ghost in sad communion dwell.

274. O thou my voice inspire,
Who touched Isaiah's hallowed lips with fire !

275. What shall we say, since silent now is he,
Who, when he spake, all things would silent be ?

276. Scarce could they hear or see their foes,
Until at weapon-point they close.

277. Nor one of all the race was known
But prized its weal above their own.

278. For he whom royal eyes disown,
When was his form to courtiers known ?

279. And chiefs, who hostage for their clan,
   Were each from home a banished man.

280. Whose castle is his helm and shield,
   His lordship the embattled field.

281. And then she wept, and then she sung—
   She sung!—the voice in better time
   Perchance to harp or lute might chime.

282. Like the leaves of the forest, when summer is green,
   That host, with their banners, at sunset was seen.

283. Each looked to sun, and stream, and plain,
   As what they ne'er might see again.

284. Praise from a friend, or censure from a foe,
   Are lost on hearers who our merits know.

285. It seems that he had never before had the good fortune
   to have seen one.

286. His administration was undoubtedly the least oppres-
   sive of that of any of the French Generals in the
   Peninsula.

287. It may put him in the way of commencing aright, and
   inspiring him to continue his researches into the
   principles of Education.

288. Students who have partially completed their studies
   elsewhere, and having satisfactory evidence of the
   fact, will be placed in advanced classes.

289. I expect that in a short time I will be in a position to
   fully acquaint the public of the reasons of this
   action on his part.

290. C. & E. return thanks to their friends and the public
   generally for their liberal support in the past, and
   we wish one and all a happy and prosperous New
   Year.

291. In short, he has received such instruction, and had such
   practice as enables him to begin aright for himself
   when he goes into a school, and further serves as a
   guide to direct his future studies.

292. A sleigh is cheaper, and much easier constructed than
   a waggon, and besides there are plenty of farmers
   which cannot get to market except in winter.

293. If you had only have went a little closer you would
   have seen that it wasn't her.

294. Specimens of these articles have been exhibited at the
different Provincial Fairs, and attracted a good deal
of attention.

295. If he is entitled to praise for withdrawing the book as
soon as his attention was drawn to it, he would have
been entitled to more if there was no necessity for
its withdrawal.

296. Among the spectators several of the fair sex were con-
spicuous, and whose smiles always makes such
meetings more agreeable.

297. There was, at the time, in the pockets of the jacket a
purse and a pair of kid gloves.

298. Alarmed by these reports it was decided to evacuate
the fort that night.

299. Macaulay wrote his history with the twofold purpose
of clearing the name of the Whigs from the charges
made by Hume, and to set forth the real life of the
English people.

300. If the patent has issued in error, or that the Commis-
sioner has been misled, or for other good cause, the
Court of Chancery has power to declare such patent
void.

301. The Detroit University is open to all who desire a
thorough medical education, of either sex.

302. The University has for the special benefit of their students enlisted an able corps of lecturers.

303. Intending matriculants are referred to the Register, (?)
Professor Siggins, who will give each all instructions
and information desired to fully acquaint them with
the requirements.

304. There is connected with the University a Free Dispen-
sary, where all who desire can take treatment, free
of cost.

305. The University will furnish scholarship certificates for
one hundred and fifteen dollars, that will entitle its
beneficiary to a full course of lectures and instruction.

309. The fee must be paid in advance to the Treasurer, who
will enter the name, and give each a ticket that will
entitle the holder to, &c.

307. Diseases of the mouth and its contiguous parts will
receive its due attention.

308. This will afford a fine means of determining the diagnostic conditions, and to observe the sanative effects of the remedies given.

309. He must possess the knowledge of a three years' course of instruction, as is taught in the University.

310. No one could choose his remedy from the botanical museum around him unless he first becomes acquainted with botanical forms.

311. The University will incorporate in its curriculum of study recognized standard medical, surgical, and scientific authority, as is indorsed by the best schools in America and Europe, and open their doors to all who, &c.

312. Soon he finds out that something is wrong, but he does not know what it is, nor where it is, and then another, and so on until his fine machine has lost its force, and all is a prey to the howling storms, and are lost in the vortex, &c.

313. The choice being left to the Trustees whether to make the change or not has created a good deal of confusion.

314. Under its influence we do things which we would be sorry to do, otherwise.

315. Having received notice to vacate our present premises, and in order to do so, we have decided to get rid of, &c.

316. A man who had been crucified, and risen again, was the centre of their hope, their joy, their affection, their confidence.

317. George III.'s reign was the most eventful and longest in British history.

318. Not being capable of examining the original, or so nearly incapable that they are averse to the effort, they run off on the line of thought first suggested.

319. He will be surprised to see the monster whom he thought was slain coming to life again, like one of those champions in the Vaihalla who was no sooner slain than he arose to his feet ready to renew the contest.

320. A. B. begs to announce that he has purchased from C. D. his entire stock and will continue the business at the old stand. Having bought the goods for cash, and as I intend to sell for cash, I will be in a position to offer bargains to my customers.

4

321. Any man or woman that once buys anything from us are sure to become regular customers.

322. You can omit the names of any whom you know will not be present at it.

323. Our Board has set a good example by dealing in a liberal spirit with the teachers in their employ.

324. I came to the conclusion that the first time I would see them I would thoroughly examine them.

325. I have examined G's Revised and Improved System of Penmanship, and I shall advise all the pupils of this school to purchase them only.

326. The worthy Principal, with his staff of able assistants, are well deserving the compliments paid them.

327. Mr. M. refused, and stated that he was going back to C., in the most peremptory manner.

328. It is well understood that five men can transact business just as satisfactorily, and certainly more expeditiously than forty or fifty.

329. A majority of our Third Class teachers, after having taught for three years, are unable to obtain a Second Class Certificate, and in consequence of which are compelled to quit the profession.

330. This is one of the few subjects that seems to be thoroughly taught in our schools.

331. Nothing can justify his resort to it so frequently.

332. There are two wheels, the one of which moves too fast, and the other too slow.

333. Some Jews in Hungary are accused of having murdered a Christian girl and using her blood to mix with their Passion bread.

334. I would not have thought that he would be so simple as to have believe such a story.

335. Another artist has been engaged of equally high reputation to finish the work.

936. It is so prepared that a patient can take it without disgust until they are permanently benefited.

337. The State has a right to see that parents should so manage their children that they should not become a burden on it.

338. We would advise you to consult your physician about it, as they are our special agents in promoting the sale.

339. A full description, it will be remembered, was given in
our last Saturday's issue, of this remarkable structure.

340. And thence delight, disgust, or cold indifference rise.

341. But scant three miles the band had rode
When o'er a height they passed.

342. Where water, clear as diamond spark,
In a stone bason fell.

343. Till through the British world was known
The names of Pitt and Fox alone.

344. Down to the Tweed his band he drew.
And muttered as the flood they view.

345. Whatever sprightly juice or tasteful food
On the green bosom of this earth are found.

346. Charge full on Scotland's central host
Or Victory and England's lost.

347. Yet oft, in holy writ we see
Even such weak minister as me
May the opposer bruise.

348. But scarce could trust my eyes
When sudden in the ring I view
A mounted champion rise.

349. For each man that could draw a sword
Had marched that morning with their lord,
Earl Adam Hepburn,--he who died
On Flodden, by his sovereign's side.

350. We recommend that occasional conferences with In-
spectors be held in connection with the practical
work of education, and thus secure the expressed
wishes of those engaged in the work.

351. Resolved: That the Council desires to express its sense
of the great loss the town has sustained by his death,
and as a mark of respect for his memory do now adjourn.

352. That the Senate, at this its first meeting since his
death, record their sorrow at the loss the province
has sustained.

353. The undersigned being desirous to clear off the balance
of his stock of summer goods in order to make room
for my steady increasing business will offer the
whole of my stock in such lots as may suit intending purchasers, and at such prices that cannot be
approached by any in the town.

PART III.

STYLE.

MISUSED WORDS.

I.—CONFOUNDING WORDS OF SIMILAR SOUND OR ORIGIN.

EXERCISE XXX.

1. His story does seem rather incredulous.
2. I have been creditably informed that such is the case.
3. It would be impossible to predicate the result of such a contest.
4. He found them in want of the commonest necessities of life.
5. All his efforts to secure an equitable distribution of heat failed.
6. Be careful not to confuse these two words.
7. They are among our most valuable contributors.
8. He stands high in the list of fictitious writers.
9. He agreed not to offer a fictitious opposition to the Government.
10, The bodies were so disfigured as to render their identity difficult.
11. He was doomed to expatiate his crimes on the gallows.
12. I hope you may succeed in convicting him of his error.
13. How will the new Regulations effect your school.
14. It was proposed to erect a statute in his honor.
15. He depreciated the attempt made by the last speaker to excite a prejudice against the company.
16. He was allowed to pursue his ordinary avocation in peace.
17. The observation of these simple rules would have prevented all difficulty.

WRONG FORMS OF WORDS.

18. It is said to be a sure preventative of ague.
19. His remarks were quite irrevalent.
20. He regarded it as a very underhanded proceeding,
21. A cursorary glance might not reveal the fact.
22. He was looked upon as a progedy of learning.
23. He went to see the tradegy of McBeth played.
24. He seemed to regard it as a clever stragetic movement.
25. He recommended it to us as an excellent dentrifice.
26. A suppositious copy. A box of blackening. I had just as leave.

II.—CONFOUNDING SYNONYMES, OR WORDS OF RELATED MEANING.

EXERCISE XXXI.

1. He seemed disposed to question the veracity of my statements.
2. He was not conscious of what had been done in his absence.
3. Tomatoes are said to be very healthy food.
4. I could not persuade him that he was wrong.
5. Did you send a verbal, or a written message?
6. In that way you will be more liable to get at the truth.
7. You may esteem yourself fortunate if you escape so easily.
8. Doubtless the story was invented for the purpose of injuring his character.
9. After a considerable interval had transpired he returned to the office.
10. In the meantime important events were transpiring in England.
11. Two hundred dollars a year is scarcely sufficient compensation for his services.
12. Her future life is said to have been virtuous and irreproachable.
13. I never saw such a quantity of sheep at a show before.

14. Such carelessness is calculated to leave a very unfavorable impression on the minds of the examiners.

15. All these things require to be taken into deliberation by the committee.

16. Had this been done their object would doubtless have been successful

17. The enormity of the cost of the proposed tunnel seemed to startle him.

18. His awkward handling of the oars showed that he was only an amateur.

19. The discovery of the telescope rendered it a comparatively easy task.

20. You will be very apt to find him in the billiard room.

21. The great bulk of the scholars belong to the village.

22. The balance of the pupils are reading in the Fourth Book.

23. The whole family enjoy a rather bad reputation—enjoy very poor health

24. The death of the veteran journalist is hourly anticipated.

25. There is no doubt that his death was hastened by the blows administered by the policeman.

26. The rule is a good enough one, but I doubt its application to the case before us.

27. We placed every thing in the office at their disposition.

28. The conscience of the purity and disinterestedness of his motives consoled him for his defeat.

III.—MISCELLANEOUS EXAMPLES OF MISUSED WORDS.

EXERCISE XXXII.

1. Such trustees perish the best interests of their school.

2. Parents require to have this idea transmuted into their minds.

3. These reports will enable parents to judge of the progression of their children.

4. With such facilities for filling the ranks of inefficient teachers there should be no difficulty in, &c.

5. The claim that it (U. C. College) can be substituted by our High Schools and Collegiate Institutes is false.

6. To this institution (U. C. C.) most of our prominent public men are indebted for their abilities.

7. This proud position has proceeded from small beginnings.

8. He says that he never saw the letter till it was published, a fact which I can prove to be false.

9. It (phonetic spelling) would make foreigners learn our language more easily.

10. Steam enables us to perform a voyage sooner than formerly

11. You want to be very careful to explain this point clearly.

12. You have the right to give me half of the road.

13. The above is a vile fabrication, actuated by the puny jealousy of our contemporary.

14. The book is full of valuable information from lid to lid.

15. I have constantly met with just such cases in my visits to the schools.

16. The issue of the campaign was still being expected by Cicero with considerable anxiety, though with little hope that the republic would be able to resume its independence.

17. He agreed to return it inside of ten days.

18. He can't take care of himself, let alone the children.

19. We came across an instance of it in our lesson this morning.

20. Feeling very dry after my walk I asked for a drink of water.

21. By so doing he imputes the veracity of the secretary.

22. The *orichalcum* of antiquity seems to have been a fictitious substance, not a natural metal.

23. Political geography is well taught, but due preponderance is not given to Mathematical and Physical.

24. It will be seen, therefore, that there is no lack of means for supplying any deficiencies that may take place in their ranks.

CHOICE OF WORDS.

EXERCISE XXXIII.

WHICH OF THE ITALICIZED WORDS OR EXPRESSIONS IN THE
FOLLOWING SENTENCES ARE PREFERABLE?

1. He had *partly (partially)* finished the work when we left.
2. In what *part (portion)* of the town does he live?
3. The letter was addressed to the *Reverent (Reverend)* Mr. Smith.
4. The children behaved in a very *reverent (reverend)* manner.
5. He thanked them for the honor *bestowed (conferred)* on him.
6. He bore the operation with the greatest *courage (fortitude)*.
7. Shall I *peel (pare)* this apple—orange—for you?
8. I would have gone if it had been *ever (never)* so stormy.
9. He ought to be put in a *straight (strait)* jacket.
10. He set before them a most *luxurious (luxuriant)* banquet.
11. What method of *proceeding (procedure)* would you adopt in such a case?
12. I never heard *such an eloquent (so eloquent a)* speech.
13. I heard it from our *mutual (common)* friend.
14. Were your instructions *oral (verbal)* or written?
15. He soon acquired the *custom (habit)* of using opium.
16. He insisted on the prompt *observance (observation)* of the regulations.
17. Don't leave any more than you *can (can't)* help.
18. The goods are to be sold *at (by)* auction to-morrow.
19. He lives *on (in)* Elgin Street.
20. He professed great sympathy *with (for)* them.
21. The counter was covered with a *various (varied)* assortment of cards.
22. His face assumed a *deadly (deathly)* paleness.
23. The *falseness (falsity—falsehood)* of his statement was soon evident.
24. The *whole (entire)* floor is covered with it.

EXERCISE XXXIV.

IMPROVE THE FOLLOWING SENTENCES BY SUBSTITUTING CORRECT
   FORMS OF EXPRESSION FOR SUCH AS ARE WRONG, OR OF
   DOUBTFUL PROPRIETY:

1. I have every confidence in his honesty.
2. You had no call to leave it within his reach.
3. He wasn't injured any, as far as I cou'd see.
4. Do you mind what I told you last day?
5. He as good as offered to take them both.
6. He got left behind by the train this morning.
7. Don't let on that you see him.
8. He wasn't quite so bad when we left.
9. He was noways to blame for the accident.
10. We drove over the bridge just before the ice struck it.
11. We waited a little it to see what he would do.
12. He vowed that he had forgotten all about it.
13. He waited quite a spell in the hope of seeing them.
14. I lit on a similar instance this morning.
15. It is rather better than a month since he left.
16. Did you make out to find where he lived?
17. He seemed to be thoroughly posted on such matters.
18. I thought it a pity of him to have to go alone.
19. He seemed to feel rather put out about it.
20. He nearly got into a scrape yesterday.
21. It isn't above a fortnight since we saw him.
22. I need a new brush the worst way.
23. I can scarcely tell them apart.
24. He is in a worse fix now than he ever was.
25. Are you done with the ruler now?
26. He never named the matter to us.
27. He promised to come right away.
28. He will blame it on you.
29. He has just got over a second attack.
30. Are you not through your dinner yet?

EXERCISE XXXV.

DISTINGUISH BETWEEN THE FOLLOWING:

1. He was unable to construe (construct) a sentence.
2. That is a very ingenious (ingenuous) explanation.
3. Divers (diverse) methods of accomplishing it were proposed.
4. He purposed (proposed) to unite the two classes.
5. It may possibly affect (effect) the desired result.
6. He suggested a practical (practicable) method of accomplishing it.
7. He told them to bring (fetch) their books.
8. She failed in her efforts to conciliate (reconcile) them.
9. He spoke contemptuously (contemptibly) of the President.
10. He made three successful (successive) attempts to reach it.
11. He referred (alluded) to it in his sermon.
12. The narrative is genuine (authentic).
13. He said he would come to-morrow (on the morrow).
14. He regarded it as a politic (political) scheme.
15. He alone can do it. He can do it alone.
16. I was reading a serial (serious) story.
17. Only one did the deductions. One did the deductions only.
18. She is at least as tall as you (as tall as you at least).
19. They won a decided (decisive) victory.
20. One is very likely (liable) to be deceived.
21. A vacant house. An empty house.
22. The entire outfit. A complete outfit.
23. The testimony (evidence) was published.
24. The victim of a delusion (an illusion).
25. Sanitary (sanatory) measures.

EXERCISE XXXVI.

EXPRESS THE FOLLOWING IN SIMPLER AND MORE NATURAL LANGUAGE.

1. The majority of the residents of the locality.
2. The unmistakable precursor.
3. The extreme felicity.
4. An exceedingly opulent individual.
5. A condition of complete indigence.
6. His customary beverage.
7. Participate in the pecuniary advantages.
8. Encountered an elderly individual.
9. Arrived in close proximity.
10. To lead to the hymeneal altar.
11. Made the recipient of the grateful acknowledgments.
12. An individual evidently identified with the agricultural interests.
13. Proceeded to his residence.
14. The services of the nearest physician were called into requisition.
15. His immortal spirit had quitted its earthly habitation.
16. The conflagration attracted an immense concourse of spectators.
17. To arrest the progress of the devouring element.
18. The assembled populace commenced to evince a disposition to, &c.
19. The unprecedented inclemency of the weather necessitated its postponement.
20. Endeavored to conceal his repugnance.
21. Sustained a fracture of the clavicle.
22. It will in all human probability eventuate in.
23. To institute a comparison between the two.
24. To inaugurate the contest.
25. At the earliest practicable period.

AMBIGUITY.

I.—FROM THE USE OF WORDS THAT MAY BEAR DIFFERENT MEANINGS.

EXERCISE XXXVII.

1. You don't seem to like anything that I do.
2. The scouts reported that they had discovered certain indications of the presence of Indians in the vicinity.
3. I can't find one of my books.
4. I did not promise to accept any offer.
5. He observed that the attendance was smaller than usual.
6. He ate a little pie for dinner.
7. Common sense, Mr. Chairman, is what I want.
8. Did you see the door open?   The window broken?
9. You have given me no easy question to answer.
10. The word is not used only by the uneducated.
11. He said that the mosquitoes would climb up on the trees and bark ; that they were very large, and that he had no doubt a great many of them would weigh a pound.

II.—FROM THE CARELESS USE OF PRONOUNS.

EXERCISE XXXVIII.

1. He told his friend that if he did not feel better in half an hour he thought he had better return.
2. Old English poetry was very different from what it is now.
3. When very little snow falls, or when it is blown off the fields, it greatly diminishes the crop of fall wheat the next season.
4. The party of Union and Progress is as superior to the Grits in political morality as they are in patriotism and statesmanship.
5. There is a mortgage on the property, which may cause some trouble.
6. A's money is equal to half of B's, which is $500.

7. She sent her back for her shawl, which she had forgotten to bring,
8. Men look with an evil eye upon the good that is in others, and think that their reputation obscures them, and that their commendable qualities do stand in their light; and therefore they do what they can to cast a cloud over them, that the bright shining of their virtues may not obscure them.

III.—FROM ELLIPSIS.

EXERCISE XXXIX.

1. I have no more control over him than others.
2. The poor think themselves no more disgraced by taking bribes than the rich by offering them.
3. He liked to hear her talk better than any of his associates.
4. He owes a good many more than you.
5. Twelve years ago he came to this town with but one shirt to his back, and now he is worth thousands.
6. The woodshed and contents of Mr. A., O——, was burned last Sunday morning.
7. He wished for nothing more than a dictionary.
8. That is a likeness of the man that painted our house and his wife.

IV.—FROM THE MISPLACEMENT OF WORDS OR CLAUSES.

EXERCISE XL.

1. And thus the son the fervent sire addressed.
2. The Duke yet lives that Henry shall depose.
3. I was not aware that you had been absent till yesterday.
4. He is only quarrelsome when he is drunk.
5. Under the circumstances I must admit that you acted fairly.
6. John Keats, the second of four children, like Chaucer and Spenser, was born in London.

7. Such is the depravity of the world that guilt is more likely to meet with indulgence than misfortune.
8. I came very near losing my way several times.
9. One of our town sportsmen shot 15 brace of partridges, along with a friend, on Saturday last.
10. A few minutes are required after giving the order, to ensure a hot breakfast, which might otherwise seem an unnecessary delay.
11. Whom chance misled his mother to destroy.
12. We import our coffee direct through our agents in New York, which is roasted and ground on the premises daily.

MISCELLANEOUS EXAMPLES OF AMBIGUITY.

EXERCISE XLI.

1. The service was impressive, but it lacked either grandeur or beauty.
2. Metal types were now introduced, which before this had been made of wood.
3. Rich or poor, you have always been a true friend to me·
4. I thought that the safest plan was to praise everything he did.
5. After some difficulty we reached the gate where we parted from our friend.
6. The next winter which I spent in town happened to be a very mild one.
7. Not a single failure has occurred, in consequence of the change in the law.
8. It will be very convenient for those who want access to the original manuscripts.
9. A man who has lost his eyesight has, in one sense, less consciousness than he had before.
10. A young man in Ottawa took creosote for the toothache, which nearly poisoned him.

11. I leave my property to my brother and his children in succession.

12. I think you will find my Latin exercise at least as good as his.

13. The vegetables and roots of all kinds surpassed all expectations, owing to its having been an unusually dry season.

14. The child that wrote the following composition had been nearly six years at school when my attention was drawn to it.

15. At the meeting last night Mr. A. was nominated to contest the riding in the Reform interest, amidst the greatest enthusiasm.

16. He was taking a view from a window of the cathedral at Lichfield in which a party of Royalists had entrenched themselves.

17. They were persons of very moderate abilities, even before they were weakened by their excesses.

18. And when it was told Saul he sent other messengers, and they prophesied likewise.

19. It was never intended, as Mr. M. has told you, that the award was not to be adopted unless ratified by the Dominion Parliament.

20. He will scarcely be consoled for the loss which he has sustained by the defeat of the by-law.

21. I said that he was a liar, it is true, and I am sorry for it.

22. That boy says he knows more than his teacher.

23. Whom should I meet, walking along King Street, but my old friend Brown.

24. Whoever is found on these premises, stealing nuts, destroying trees, or otherwise, will be prosecuted according to law.

25. The essential elements of a noble manhood are developed only by the personal contact and influence of the true teacher upon the scholar, and this is one of the defects of our system of secondary education.

26. An eye witness says he saw him bring down a brace of pheasants which rose together unexpectedly in a small cover, each with a single ball from a double-barrelled rifle.

OBSCURITY.

I.—USE OF TECHNICAL, OR UNCOMMON TERMS.

II.—CIRCUMLOCUTION, OR VERBOSITY.

III.—USE OF LONG PARENTHESES.

IV. —WANT OF UNITY, RESULTING IN LONG AND INVOLVED
SENTENCES.

*N.B.—For obvious reasons it has not been thought worth
while to give a formal exercise on this fault.   Two or three
illustrations are, however, subjoined.*

1.—He found on examination a contusion of the integuments
under the orbit, with an extravasation of blood and
ecchymosis of the surrounding cellular tissue, which
was in a tumefied state, and also with a slight abra-
sion of the cuticle.

2.—As man is a microcosm, in whom all the grand principles
of the universe converge, making him the essence of
their combined action, an epitome of the whole, com-
bining as he does in the elements of his composition
those substances that are governed by the same rul-
ings as other organized bodies, differing only in its
psychological powers and its ability to answer the
telegrams of nature addressed to his senses and con-
ceptions, and contemplate the great harmonium of
the universe with his worthy self as the crown of all
its ultimates.

3.—The children in our elementary schools are capable of
acquiring elementary teaching, without any fear that
either their physical or mental energies will be over-
tasked to an extent which, under the favorable conditions in which our community is happily placed,
we can safely venture upon, in comparison with any
other community, provided modes of teaching in
harmony with nature's laws are required to prevail,
and thus aiding and strengthening the child's mental
and physical development.

WANT OF FORCE OR HARMONY.

EXERCISE XLII.

I.—USE OF UNNECESSARY WORDS.

1. Hence you will see, therefore, he must necessarily be in error.
2. Several of the spectators who were present voluntarily offered to assist him.
3. He suffered great anxiety of mind in the interval that intervened between his application and their decision.
4. What was the subject matter of his discourse?
5. He brought the work to a final completion yesterday.
6. Remember that the period of youth is the time to form correct habits.
7. They will soon have an entire monopoly of the whole trade.
8. It has been our uniform and invariable practice to do so.
9. That seems to be the universal opinion of all that have seen it working.
10. In addition to these there must be added the following names.
11. I never was so astonished before in the whole course of my existence.
12. It generally happens that there are nearly always some absent.
13. After conversing together for a few moments they both rose up and left the room.
14. Somebody or other had covered it over during his absence.
15. We had to listen to their mutual recriminations.

II.—Too many Connectives.   Too many Statements in one Sentence.

EXERCISE XLIII.

1. He went up to him, and awakened him gently, and drew him back from the edge of the·precipice, and saved his life.

2. He called his boy but got no answer, so he searched as far as his chains would permit, but could not find him, so at last he became frantic, and tried to break his chains, but he could not.

3. He asked her to show him her album, which she did, and she called his attention to the likeness of one young lady with whom she had been very intimate when she was attending the Normal School, and who has since attracted attention by her paintings, some of which were exhibited at the Exhibition which was held in T. last fall.

4. When Alexander took Sidon he left his generals to appoint a king, so they went to two brothers and asked one of them to be king, but neither of them would accept, for they said that they were no relation to any former king, and that it would not be right for them to reign, but they told the generals of a man named Abdalonymus, who was related to their former king, but who was so poor that he had to keep a market garden so as to gain a livelihood.

EXERCISE LXIV.

III.—WEAK ENDINGS. BAD ARRANGEMENT. LOOSE STRUCTURE.

1. It was a practice which he could learn nothing of the origin of.
2. His conduct was exceedingly imprudent, to say the least of it.
3. It is an undertaking which the whole community will reap the benefit of, if he succeeds in it.
4. It is a much more elaborate and costlier structure than there was any need of.
5. He divided all his property in his life time equally among his three sons to avoid any disputes or law suits.
6. He called a meeting of the principal shareholders at his office, secretly, that evening. at the suggestion of the secretary, to consider the matter.

EXERCISE XLV.

IV.—REPETITION OF THE SAME, OR SIMILAR SOUNDS.

1. He exemplified the principal applications of the principle by numerous examples.
2. Each of these Forms was formerly divided into two divisions.
3. It is very desirable that all those who desire to compete should be present.
4. It was quite clear to all present that he did not clearly understand the question.
5. He described it in an uninteresting manner.
6. He certainly acted extremely cautiously.
7. I have had occasion to pass the house on several occasions recently.
8. We had never seen, or even imagined such a scene.
9. He used many expressions not usually used by good writers.

ERRORS IN THE USE OF FIGURATIVE LANGUAGE.

I.—INAPPROPRIATE METAPHORS.

II.—IMPROPER MINGLING OF METAPHOR AND LITERAL STATEMENT.

III.—MIXED METAPHORS.

EXERCISE XLVI.

1. The *magnum opus* of education is creeping up the steep ascent of efficiency.
2. The questions will naturally partake of the same complexion as his teaching.
3. The memory is nourished to fulness, but the reason, judgment and understanding do not get their daily bread ; they are treated as orphans of the mind.
4. It should be the prayer of every noble minded man that the gray dawn of the morning may fade into the brilliant sunlight of noon.
5. The heroic Spanish gunners had no defence but bags of cotton, joined to their own insuperable courage.
6. He flung his powerful frame into the saddle and his great soul into the cause.
7. The building was surrounded by a mob armed with rustic weapons and ungovernable fury.
8. They were the seven pillars of the new House of Wisdom in the wilderness. In August, 1639, these seven pillars assembled, possessing for the time full power.
9. Our contemporary fancied that he smelled a very large mouse, and in his greediness he was determined to possess it.
10. Now from my fond embrace by tempest torn,
    One other column of the state is borne,
    Nor took a kind adieu, nor sought consent.
11. No human happiness is so serene as not to contain some alloy.

12. At length Erasmus curbed the wild torrent of a barbarous age.

13. The colonies were not yet ripe to bid adieu to British connection.

14. A torrent of superstition consumed the land.

15. Hope, the balm of life, darts a ray of light into the thick gloom.

16. We must keep the ball rolling, till it becomes a thorn in their sides

17. There is not a single view of human nature that is not sufficient to extinguish the seeds of human pride.

18. In a moment the thunderbolt was upon them, deluging their country with invaders.

19. I bridle in my struggling muse in vain,
That longs to launch into a bolder strain.

20. On they went, past fertile fields, past vine-clad slopes, halting now and then at young clearings, the abode of the few who had come to lay the corner stones of future cities on the placid bosom of the broad Ohio.

21. Irregularity of attendance is a log and chain on the progress of instruction, for it blasts and withers the noblest purposes of the best of teachers.

22. There are many considerations which enable me to state that the wave of progress is flowing on to the maturity of perfection.

23. Many embark in the profession without training, experience, or adaptation, and having neither compass nor rudder to guide them, they steer for no particular harbour. This leakage can only be stopped by paying teachers adequate salaries.

24. The knowledge thus acquired, being associated with reason, would not be a passing cloud, and being resident in them it would serve as a pilot to their judgments in solving the problems of life.

25. But although clouds of dusky warriors were seen from time to time hovering on the highlands, as if watching their progress they experienced no interruption.

26. If no authority, not in its nature temporary, were allowed to one human being over another, society would not be employed in building up propensities with one hand which it has to curb with another.

MISCELLANEOUS ERRORS OF GRAMMAR AND STYLE.

EXERCISE XLVII.

1. The reading of the Misses Alice and Mary C., and Master Samuel A., were deserving of special eulogism.

2. The author has kept in mind that clergymen, more than those of any other profession, were likely to study this treatise.

3. Phonetic spelling might obscure the derivation of words, but being that scarcely one out of every hundred persons care about derivation, it would not matter much.

4. Your committee beg to report that they have carefully considered the plans, which we herewith submit for your consideration, and would recommend them for adoption.

5. The desire of wealth, or the desire of equalizing or surpassing others, are, neither of them, in themselves either virtuous or vicious.

6. A perfect alphabet of the English language, and of every other language, would contain a number of letters equal to the distinct elementary sounds it contained.

7. Parties having building material laying around cannot be too careful about having it close to the road as serious consequences might ensue.

8. He was blamed for pardoning criminals whom public opinion asserted should have expatiated their crimes on the gallows.

9. In this manner we can get news from all parts of the world in a few hours that formerly took days.

10. Bills are requested to be paid quarterly.

11. All hands up that can answer the question.

12. Probably no modern invention, except steam, has done so much for man as the telegraph.

13. Faith in dreams, and in other such superstitions, was carried to a great extent in former times.

14. Miss Lucy D. returned from M. on Saturday, where she is engaged in teaching, on account of the illness of her father.

15. If any reader"thinks that I have devoted too much space to this part of my subject, I can only say that I have done so intentionally.

16. The amount was subscribed by a few individuals, among whom I find the names of A. and B.

17. Such deviations have not been made without due care and attention being paid to the conflicting opinions of different writers.

18. The writer was further told that if he had anything to say against the book, why did he not come out boldly in print and say it.

19. Worse than all, not one page of the two editions correspond. We have adopted the paging of the first edition, because it is most likely to be in the hands of readers.

20. We would willingly add it to Dr. Hincks' collection of Canadian curiosities, than which we venture to affirm none more curious is at present in the worthy Professor's possession.

21. He should be led to understand that he enjoys the scorn and contempt of all honest people.

22. The Board and its officers will be careful to make no entries on the above ; or to delay their report after the 20th of January.

23. Nowhere are incredulous blunders to be met with more than in the composition of advertisers.

24. The friends thou hast, and their adoption tried, Grapple them to thy soul with hooks of steel.

25. Canada has arrived to such a state of depression that every day brings new disasters, amounting to the sum of $22,000,000 for the last twelve months.

26. There are no people on the earth, except the Chinese, which have any claim to be called civilized, who are such slaves to local limitations as the French.

27. He undertook to show that the effect of the regulations would be to increase the quality of the pupils, as well as their quantity.

28. Board and lodging is found by chance during the time the character is being formed, without little or any judicious supervision.

29. The wants of our educational system were pressing, and had to be speedily met, as well as defects removed, and improvements supplied.

30. There is also many questions taken to him by the children in Arithmetic which he fails to tell them how to do, and cannot do them himself.

31. It teaches the right use of our mother tongue by giving instances of the wrong use of it, and showing why they are wrong.

32. The opportunity was presented of adjusting the functions of these institutions so that the work of each should find its proper point of contact, and not overlap each other.

33. I have been told that people will not buy sewing machines, only from peddlers who will talk them into buying the kind they are selling and running down all others.

34. Any person who wants to get either of these articles, by writing me, and saying the kind of sewing machine or organ they want, and if I cannot get it for them at the wholesale price I will let them know.

35. Two substantives, when they come together and do not signify the same thing, the former must be in the possessive.

36. The fact is patent that without due examinatian, or useless because ineffective examination, the book has been sanctioned.

37. The verb is a word which states what a thing does or is done to.

38. An author who is translated in this fashion suffers as much as when Archbishop Neville was translated from York to St Andrews, by a Pope whom Scotland did not acknowledge.

39. The several hospitals are open to the students under the guidance of a corps of able professors and practitioners who will take ample pains to illustrate the same at the bedside.

40. Then if he is called to testify in a cause for homicide, he might be able to tell at least some of the probable causes of death that befall our race.

41. He searches with avidity for the hidden causes, and with his skilful hand makes loose their bonds, and frees the sufferer from its ruthful folds.

42. The vain pretender has sunk in the whirlpool of his own ruin, carrying with him the innocent and unwary, with saddened hearts to surviving friends, who are made the sad victims of their own confidence.

43. What would you think of the safety of an ocean steamer, freighted with human life, looking onward with palpitating hearts to meet dear ones in a far off land, whose engine was run by a person who could not name the parts of his machinery, or knew its capacity or the limits of its power.

44. Feeling the necessity for a more thorough system of medical training, and a more familiar acquaintance with the medical sciences and their collateral branches than is required in the prescribed course of medical studies, and the time in which to become conversant with the branches taught, as are laid down in their course by the majority of medical colleges in our country, it was deemed expedient to establish a school, &c.

45. The Kings of Denmark and Norway invaded England, and spreading themselves over the country committed many depredations.

46. In a few days I will more fully explain to you my views and claims on your suffrages, which I consider equal to any candidate which might offer himself for your approbation.

47. In both cases a customer can sit as long as he pleases, but those of the first class have also the right of taking their cups to the third storey and smoke as well as read while enjoying his drink whatever it may be.

48. Last Sunday a new programme was entered upon, printed at this office, which we think will add to the interest in its exercises.

49. After that I shall begin to think that nothing is too strange to be incredible.

50. In England we are said to learn manners at second hand from your side of the water, and that we dress our behaviour in the frippery of France.

5

51. Mr. A.   Please accept my best thanks for the very prompt and liberal settlement of my fire loss of $10.75 in full from the above company which occurred on Friday, 16th inst., four days after the occurrence to my full and entire satisfaction.

52. I will still continue to sell for cash, and no second price, thereby enabling me to offer my customers unusual good value.

53. Trusting by strict application to business, and determined to second my position by offering the best value in this county, I trust not only to retain my present large connection but a larger increase for the future.

54. They approved of the recommendation for the retirement of the Principal from his office, whom they found was desirous of retiring by reason of impaired health.

55. We are not an offensive society, but on the contrary slow to take offence and offer none, act as Christians, and no intoxicating liquor was allowed in our lodges.

56. The cultivation of the soil, the most honorable and independent industry with which men or women could be engaged, being abandoned by those best able to make it pay, impoverishes the country.

57. Not finding the cash box, which was the object of his visit, he took the key of the store from Mr. M's pocket, and repaired thither which place he ransacked pretty well.

58. He hoped the members of the order would make a note of the fact that our present Prime Minister, who had lately visited the R. C. Cathedral in Quebec, and took part in the celebration of high mass, was one of the most shameful pieces of hypocrisy that was ever perpetrated.

59. He begs to draw their attention to the fact that owing to having almost the exclusive sale of books used in the Collegiate Institute enables him to buy largely, and thereby able to give the best discount.

60. We, the undersigned electors of the ward of St. G., having viewed the government of our civic affairs for the past twelve months, the recent exposure of public documents and the failure of securing pure

and good water, as well as general improvements in the ward, demand an immediate change, and therefore having a knowledge of your business qualifications and integrity, respectfully request, &c.

61. We, the undersigned electors of St. L. ward, knowing that you have been prominently connected with the interests of the east end for many years, and being also a large ratepayer, together with many other qualifications, we deem you admirably fitted to represent our interests at the Council Board, and therefore request, &c.

62. Gentlemen, ———— Although my real estate interests in your ward being equal to many of you, I feel I would be wanting in duty if I did not appreciate the motive you had in view, and I cannot find language to express my gratitude for the intended honor to be conferred on me.

63. A truly national system of education is as much concerned in rearing up a moral and intelligent population, and securing honestly and fair dealing as essential qualities of every citizen, as well as mental culture.

64. The Committee are of opinion that the papers for the Intermeiate should be different from those for the Teachers' Examination, and so to preserve to the former its true object, of being a test for such moderate proficiency as pupils generally after the course of two years in the High School might reasonably be expected to attain, in order to pass from the lower to the upper school and the Intermediate to cease to be a barrier between the lower and upper school.

65. The college has always possessed a distinctive element in nearly one-half of its pupils being resident, and so subjected when under wholesome influences to a further process of intellectual development, and which in the experience of other countries, as well as the fiftieth year of the college itself, has been found advantageous.

66. The number of day pupils, especially in the lower forms, interfere with a larger element of resident boarders, as well as the inferior boarding house accommodation ; and the high rates paid by boarders, both for

tuition fees and board dues, and which, as one of the objects of the Provincial endowment, should be rendered more accessible to the parents of the pupils throughout the Province, who may desire to avail themselves of the special advantages afforded by the discipline and other educational influences of the College residence.

67. This pamphlet covers a broad ground, and volume after volume might be written upon it.

68. We shall be satisfied if we can throw any additional light upon a subject of such vital importance to those who are its unfortunate victims.

69. The beneficial effects of Cod Liver Oil in Consumption has become a proverb.

70. In September, 1877, my health began to fail and my physician pronounced it spinal trouble.

71. The price is one dollar per bottle, or six bottles for five dollars, and can be obtained from druggists and dealers in medicine generally throughout the United States.

72. These facts being apparent to the medical profession, and knowing, as they do, its intrinsic virtues, we have been induced by them to prepare it in an emulsion.

73. Soon after the patient commences its use the appetite and digestion are improved, and a demand is created for food that has not existed before.

74. We will guarantee from its use better results in the various diseases for which it is adapted than any single or combined remedy in existence.

75. On account of its nauseous properties and the difficulty of administering it, especially to children, where it is most useful, it has come largely into disuse and been substituted by pills and purgatives.

76. Common sense teaches if it is instrumental in curing the racking cough of the consumptive that has lasted for months, why should it not cure a cough of a few weeks duration.

77. Reason teaches us to suggest that if the patient is sensibly affected by cold, the mild and equitable climate of the South would seem to be advisable.

78. It must be borne in mind, however, that although a remedy may possess wonderful curative properties its usefulness is greatly impaired unless perfect obedience to the laws of health are conformed to.

79. We believe we are warranted in making the statement that more physicians in this country prescribe it than any other remedy known in the Materia Medica except it may be quinine.

80. We must confess to a sense of satisfaction in producing a remedy that has the entire sanction of the medical profession, as well as being almost a specific for this dreadful scourge.

81. We sincerely hope you will read carefully these pages, and if you have been fortunate enough to escape from this relentless foe, be kind enough to send it to some friend who requires the medical and life-giving properties that it presents.

82. A resolution was adopted pledging those present to murder the jurymen who convicted Louise Michel at the first opportunity.

83. Some of the younger pupils seemed to enjoy it, but to the older ones the lecture was not so appreciative as expected.

84. Mr. H. has pleasure in announcing that the following Manuals are now ready :

Male Arithmetical Questions with answers, 1s. 6d.
Female   "   "   "   "   1s. 6d.

85. Regulations. (3) A professional gardener will decide on the merits of the plants, by whom any violation of the preceding regulations will be detected, and such exhibitors will be excluded from any share in the prizes awarded.

86. Wanted, a saddle horse for a young lady, gentle and well trained. Apply at No. —, E. St.

87. Several candidates who might otherwise have earned high marks are reduced by gross errors in Ortho-graphy.

88. Parents have to suffer loss for the depredations of their children when at home, and why not abroad ?

89. Should they refuse they ought to be obliged to pay a fine, and the child chastised by a person appointed by the court.

90. An advertisement appeared in Saturday's *Mail* to the effect that there was a good opening in M. for a doctor, having no name or address attached.

91. A few friends of the deceased followed the remains to Evergreen Cemetery, where they were quietly interred in a new lot, without service or ceremony.

92. Among the many anxious eyes that saw for the first time the blue, hazy hills of the new land wherein they were to try their fortunes, was a small family group, one of which was a bright-eyed little boy of five years old.

93. I have been much pleased with the excellent papers which have appeared in the *Journal* during the past year, and for this I am sure the educational staff of Ontario as a whole are grateful.

94. This is to certify that I attended Mrs. M. in her last illness, which was caused by a fall upon the ice, and that she died in consequence thereof.

95. In no case should the body be exposed to view ; no public funeral held, and as few attend as possible.

96. As the stag fights at bay, with a heroism such as despair alone begets, so fought the Pole and his followers under the hail of bullets which sang among them.

97. During the forenoon the American gunboat *Michigan* began to patrol the river to prevent any breaches of the neutrality laws ; and shut her eyes whenever a boat with reinforcements or stores for O'Neill happened to be crossing from the American shore.

98. I would advocate the establishment of schools where children of mothers who are obliged to work the whole day to gain a livelihood for their children, and who are in the meantime abandoned on the streets, would be cared for and get their dinners and be returned to their homes in the evening, or some of the children might bring their dinners.

99. The postmaster has received a communication from a sailor near O., informing him of the death of a man named J. S., who once lived near here, by falling off their boat in a gale and getting drowned, and wished his friends to know.

100. We are told to look at the county of X. who so nobly provided a house of refuge for their poor, and it only costs that county one dollar and eighty-three cents per week for each inmate.